Forgotten Magnificence

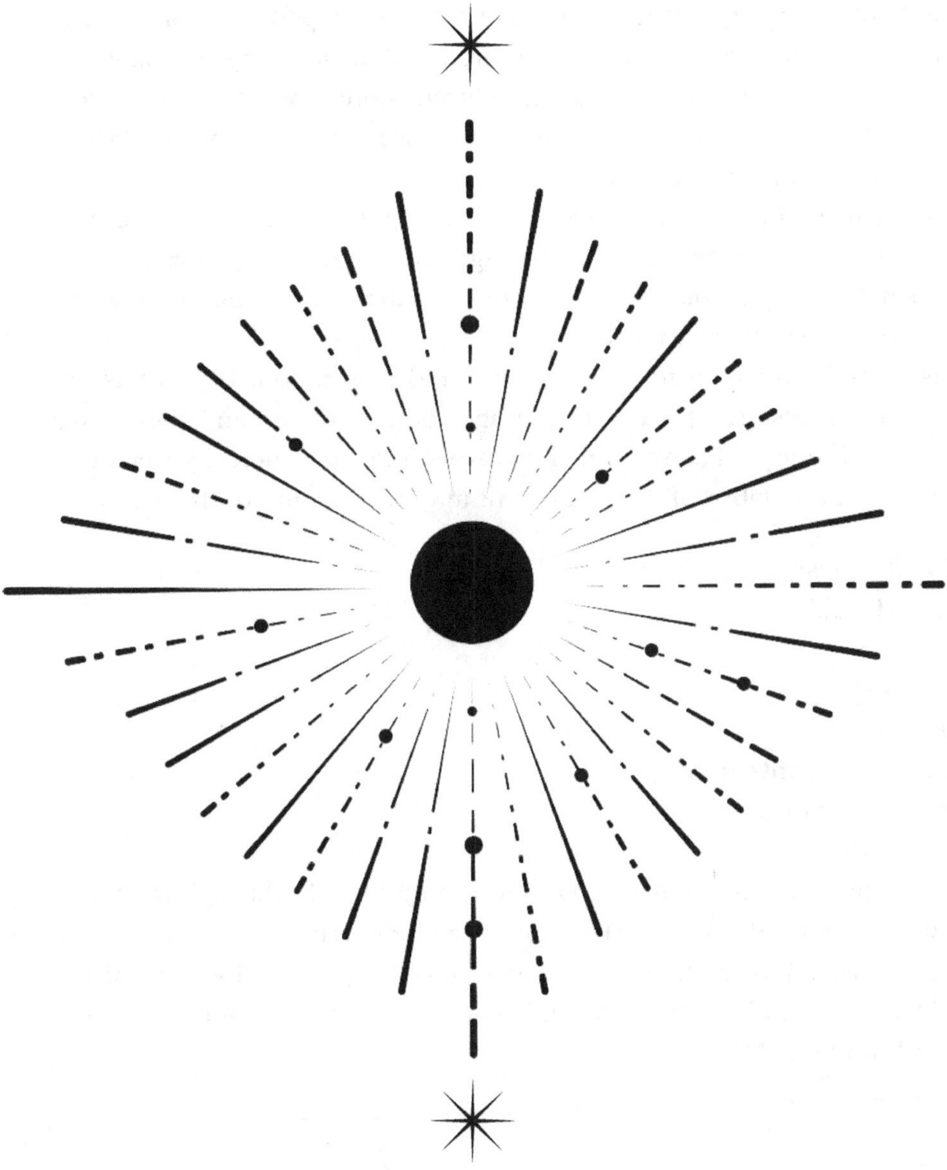

Copyright Notice ©2025 Sarah McAllorum

Rights Reserved.
Published by Sarah McAllorum
Hardcover ISBN: 978-1-0693713-1-7
Paperback ISBN: 978-1-0693713-0-0

This book, Forgotten Magnificence, including all poems, short stories, affirmations, and written content, is protected under copyright law. No part of this book may be copied, reproduced, stored, or distributed in any form—electronic, mechanical, or otherwise—without prior written permission from the author or publisher.

This includes, but is not limited to, photocopying, scanning, recording, reposting, unauthorized digital sharing, and resale. Any unauthorized reproduction or distribution of this work is a direct violation of copyright law and will be subject to legal action.

This book is intended for personal use and inspiration. If you wish to share its message, please encourage others to obtain their own authorized copy. Thank you for respecting the integrity, creative ownership, and labor of love that went into the creation of this work.

Contributors:
Editor-in-Chief
Mary Max
Cover Art
Artvitalya
Interior Art Contributors
Paladorn Rutaiwan
Victoria Rusyn

This book is a collaborative creation, brought to life through the talent and dedication of these contributors. Their expertise and artistry have helped shape Forgotten Magnificence into the powerful and inspiring collection it is today. Deep gratitude to each of them for their invaluable contributions to this work.

Dedication

To humanity—

To the seekers, the wanderers, the ones who dare to dream beyond what they have been told.

This book is for you; the one who holds these pages in your hands, drawn by something unseen but deeply felt.

This book is dedicated to those who have walked through darkness searching for light, to the ones who have fallen and risen, again and again. To those who have questioned their worth, doubted their path, or wondered if they were ever enough—let these words remind you that you are. You always were.

To the warriors of love, the holders of truth, the quiet ones whose strength has yet to be fully seen—this is for you. May these words ignite a spark, a remembrance, a return to the infinite well of power that has always lived within you.

You are a force, a light, a piece of the divine itself, walking this earth with purpose.

May this book be a sanctuary, a mirror, a beacon of truth. May it remind you of who you are beneath the heaviness of the world. May it give you permission to stand taller, love deeper, and embrace the radiance of your existence.

For you are a gift. A sacred, once-in-eternity expression of the infinite. And the world is brighter because you are here.

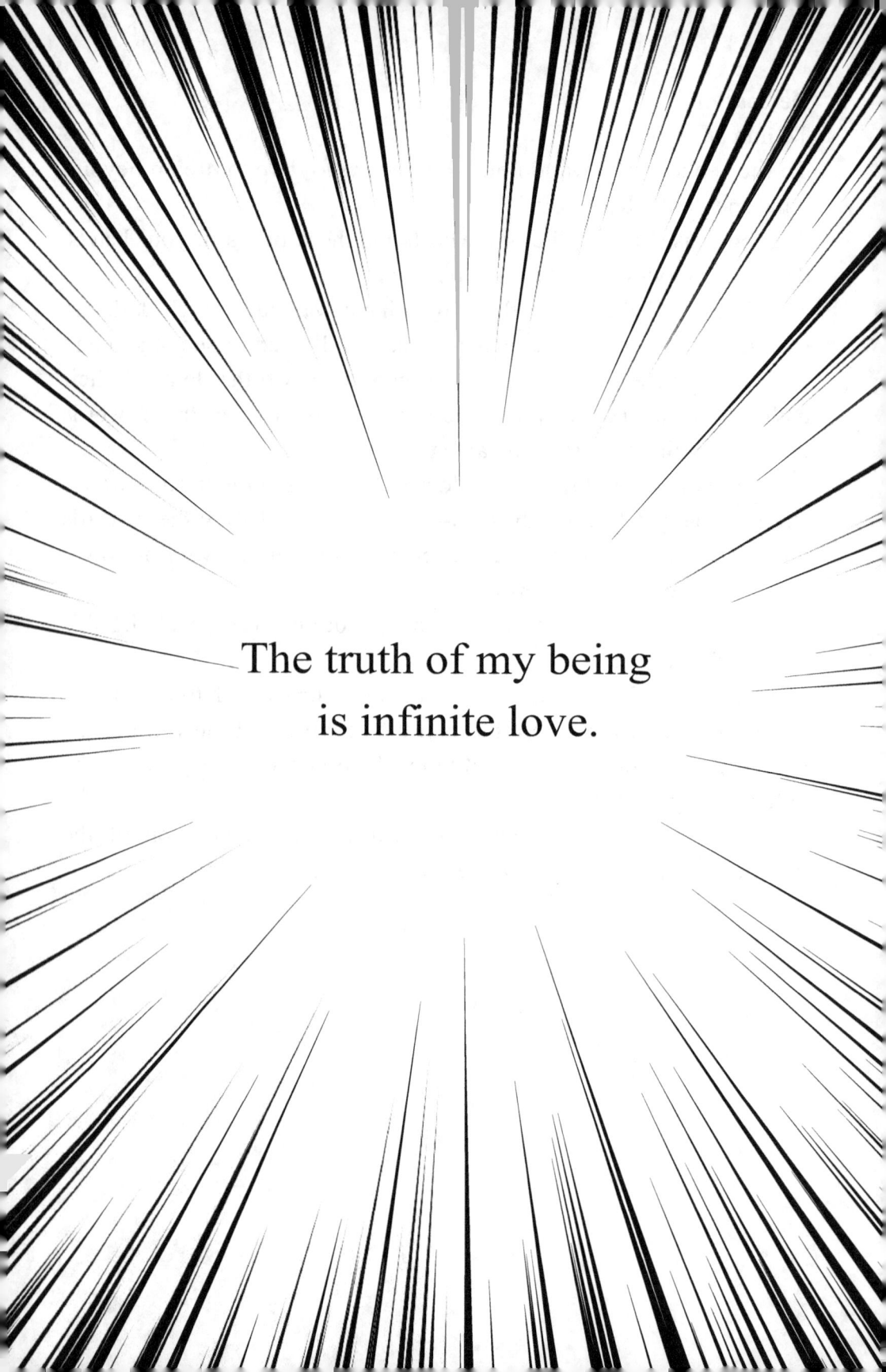

The truth of my being
is infinite love.

Table of Contents

Introduction to Forgotten Magnificence, 8
Sacred Prayer of Magnificence, 10
Before I Left Heaven (Introductory Short Story), 12
Remembrance, 17
Stand On Your Truth, 19
Take me Down Deep, 21
The Place Where We Hide, 23
Beneath The Silence, 25
Reveal You, 27
The Tender Nudge of Truth, 29
Uniquely Known, 31
The Universe Knows Your Name, 35
Happiness, 37
The Mirror of Creation, 39
Finding Freedom, 41
Diamond in the Rough, 43
Wings of Becoming, 45
Forgotten Magnificence, 47
Journey to the Blossoming Rose, 51
Arriving Is the Inevitable, 55
Letting God Do the Heavy Lifting, 57
I Didn't Come Here to Be Who You Wanted Me to Be, 59
Surrender Is Grace in Action, 61
The Guru Within, 63
I Am the Safe Space to Fall in Love with Myself, 65
There Will Never Be Another You, 67
The Sacred Song of Return, 69
The Unblemished Soul, 71
Forged in Fire, 73
No Longer Dancing in the Den of Thieves, 75
Reclaiming My Throne, 77
Close to the Bone, 79
I Am Steady, 81
Stepping Into Your Great, 83
My Abundance Flows to Me, 85
God Made No Mistake on You, 87

Let Everything in Life Inspire You, 89
God Sees What You Don't, 91
I Dance with the Heartbeat of Creation, 93
You Never Get the Same Moment Twice, 95
Worth Your Salt, 97
Golden Doorway, 99
Through the Eyes of the Divine, 101
The Day I Saw Heaven in My Own Eyes, 103
This Is Your Winning Season, 105
Heaven, Take My Breath Away, 107
Grace, Grit, and Glory, 109
The Fulfillment Within, 111
Holy Armor, 113
Holy Hands That Heal, 115
Standing in the Middle of the Zero Point, 117
Dare to Be Brave, 119
Congruency of the Heart and Mind, 121
Sometimes We Don't Get to Know Why, 123
You Are the One Who Has Come to Save Yourself, 125
Only Love Can Walk Through Fire, 127
Do Not Underestimate Your Strength, 129
When You Have Nothing to Hide You Become a Very Dangerous Human, 131
Poetic Alchemy, 133
Beyond the Surface, 135
Beyond the Dark Night, 137
Divinity in Form, 139

Forgotten Magnificence Short Stories, 142

Unshaken: The Power of Standing in Your Truth, 146
They Will Never Forget How You Made Them Feel, 152
You Can't Fix What Was Never Broken, 158
Let Me Show You Love Exists, 162
While the Embers Are Still Burning, 166
The Weight of Love, 172
The Dance of Capacity, 179
The Prayer That Was Never Lost, 184

101 Affirmations

This collection also includes a powerful section of 101 Affirmations designed to anchor you in your magnificence, realign your thoughts with truth, and empower your journey. These affirmations can be used as daily mantras, sacred prayers, or reminders of the infinite wisdom within you. Speak them, write them, embody them—let their energy reshape the way you see yourself and the world. 188

Conclusion, 196

Introduction to Forgotten Magnificence

Thank you for embarking on this sacred journey into the depths of Forgotten Magnificence. Your presence here is no accident; there is a quiet calling that has drawn you to these words, a gentle nudge from the universe inviting you to remember what has always been within you. This collection of poetry and short stories is a doorway—a space where your soul is invited to reconnect with the brilliance that time, circumstance, and the noise of the world may have buried or obscured.

This work is not merely a book of poems and short stories but an offering, crafted with care and reverence to serve as a mirror, a guide, and a source of reflection. It was born from the understanding that within each of us lies an untapped magnificence—a divine inheritance that we sometimes forget in the face of life's challenges. These words are not here to instruct or impose but to awaken and stir. They are meant to meet you wherever you are, resonating uniquely with the truths and questions that dwell within your heart.

When you encounter the word God in these pages, with love, I say this with deep care and respect—I want to make this absolutely clear—how you perceive God is entirely up to you. The word is not here to tell you what to believe, nor is it meant to impose any singular truth upon you. God in this collection is a guide toward the boundless force of creation, the essence of life itself. Whether you see this as God, Spirit, the Universe, Love, or something entirely different, allow it to be a reflection of what feels true for you. It is not about defining the divine in a rigid way, but rather, opening a space for you to step into a personal dialogue with the infinite as you understand it. There is no right or wrong way to perceive the sacred—only what resonates deeply with your heart.

Similarly, when you come across the word prayer, with love and deep respect, I want to gently offer this—prayer is what you make it. It is not about my perception of prayer, nor anyone else's, but rather what feels meaningful to you. Prayer is not confined to a single tradition, nor does it require a specific posture or spoken word. It may be the quiet moments of reflection, the deep inhale before surrender, the stillness where you meet yourself, or the gratitude you carry in your heart.

Whether it is words, silence, movement, or intention, the essence of prayer is your connection to something greater—whatever that may be for you. Trust that your way is enough, and that how you choose to commune with the sacred is entirely yours to define.

The poems and short stories you will read here are layered with metaphors, allegories, and symbolic deeper meaning—each a jewel waiting to reveal itself in its own time. This collection is intentionally crafted to allow your interpretations to take precedence, giving you the freedom to find meaning that feels authentic to your journey. I invite you to take only what resonates, what feels like truth in your soul, and lovingly leave the rest. You are the one who defines what meaning sits right with your spirit, and that is the only truth that matters.

It is my deepest hope that as you move through this book, you will feel the love and intention with which it was created. This body of work exists to uplift the spirit, to honor the cosmic consciousness that we are all part of, and to remind you of the sacred connection you have to everything around you. In the fast pace of life, we often forget the stillness, the light, and the infinite wonder that resides within. This collection is here to help you rediscover that.

Take your time. Pause, breathe, and let each word settle into the quiet places of your being. This is not a journey of the mind alone but one of the soul. Approach this work with openness, curiosity, and a willingness to remember the magnificence that has always been yours. Thank you for allowing me to walk beside you on this path of rediscovery. May these words serve as a light to guide you, a balm to comfort you, and a spark to reignite the truth of who you are. You are seen, you are loved, and you are magnificent—beyond measure and beyond words.

With deepest gratitude and love,
Sarah McAllorum

Sacred Prayer of Magnificence

God/Source/Creation,
Hover over me, fill me with Your grace and love.
Breathe life into my spirit and anchor me in the truth
Of who I am and who I am meant to be.
Allow me to receive what is in the highest alignment for me today.
Guide me to what I need to know,
What I need to see, and what I need to heal,
Moment by moment, breath by breath.
I pause now, focusing on the rhythm of my breath,
Centering my being in Your presence.
I am held, deeply and eternally,
By the infinite love that surrounds me.
Great Divine, hover over me,
Hover within my life and through my life.
Illuminate the beauty I've forgotten,
And awaken the magnificence that lives within my soul.
May I see myself through Your eyes—
Whole, worthy, and radiant.
May I dwell in Your peace,
A peace that roots me in love and rises me to freedom.
Let Your light guide my path,
Let Your love heal my wounds,
And let Your wisdom awaken my highest purpose.
With each breath, may I trust in Your divine plan,
And embrace the unfolding of my life as a sacred gift.
And so it is.

Before I Left Heaven

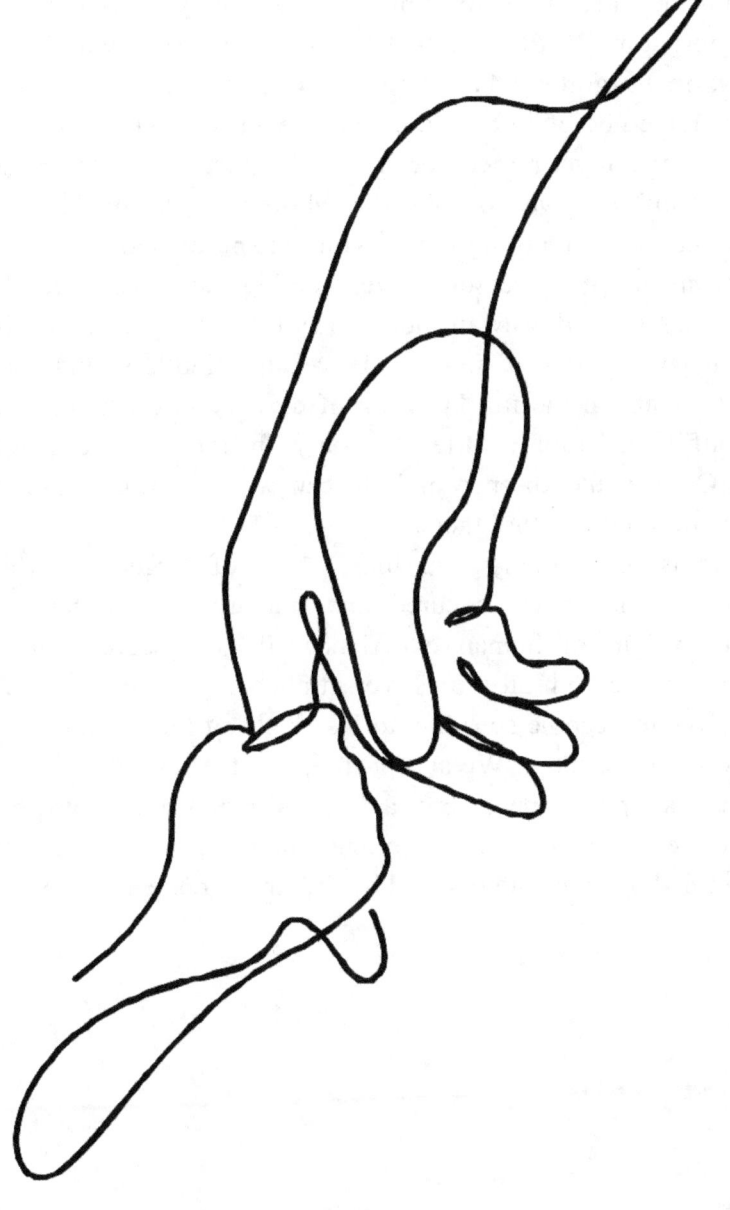

Before I Left Heaven Introduction

There is a question that lingers in the heart of every seeker: Why are we here? Why would a soul, perfect and whole, cradled in the infinite love of the Divine, ever choose to leave that sacred place to enter a world of uncertainty, suffering, and longing? What could possibly be worth the descent? What force is powerful enough to call a being from the embrace of creation itself and send it spiraling into the density of Earth?

This first short story, Before I Left Heaven, is the doorway to the journey that follows in Forgotten Magnificence. It invites you to consider that before you arrived here, before your first breath, you were something far greater than you can yet remember. You were part of the eternal, a spark of creation itself. And yet, despite the wholeness, despite the oneness, despite the peace— something within you whispered, Go.

Love has always been the reason. Love—the highest, most sacred force in existence—pulls souls downward not as a fall, but as an offering. It is the great calling that urges a soul to leave the limitless and step into limitation, to abandon the full knowing of divinity in order to experience the raw, unfiltered truth of life; for only in forgetting can we truly remember. Only in the absence of light can we seek it out and, through that seeking, illuminate it for others.

To incarnate is to willingly step into a veil of forgetting, where the memory of our origin is obscured and our true nature lies dormant beneath the weight of human experience. It is a sacred paradox: in Heaven, we are one with all things, yet in choosing to come to Earth, we allow ourselves to become separate, to lose sight of the infinite so that we may discover it once more. We accept the pain, the loss, the fear, and the struggle, not as punishment, but as an initiation into something far greater. We are sculpted by the experience of being human, tempered by hardship, refined by love, and purified by the fire of remembrance.

If you have ever felt lost, if you have ever longed for something unseen, something beyond this world—perhaps this story will awaken a knowing within you. Perhaps it will stir a memory long buried beneath the layers of time. Because the truth is, you did not come here by accident. You did not fall. You answered a call.

This story is for those who have wondered why they feel an ache they cannot name, why they have always searched for something they cannot define. It is for those who have carried a heaviness in their soul, sensing that Earth was never their first home, and yet knowing that they chose to be here anyway. It is for those who have struggled, who have wept, who have doubted their own worth, only to rise again and again, drawn forward by an unseen force that whispers, You are here for a reason.

Before I Left Heaven

The child sat on the edge of infinity, her legs dangling over a golden horizon, staring down at the spinning, chaotic beauty of Earth below. Beside her sat God, radiant and serene, His presence vast yet intimate. The two were silent for a time, gazing together at the vibrant yet fractured world.

"Father," the little girl asked, her voice soft yet filled with an innocent urgency, "Why does Earth look like that?" She pointed at the swirls of light and shadow, the bright spots surrounded by streaks of darkness.

God smiled gently. "What do you see, my child?"

"I see... hurt," she replied, her small brow furrowing. "I see people lost in the dark, and it's like they can't find their way out. Why does it have to be like that? Why do they hurt so much?"

God's eyes held infinite compassion as He looked at her. "They were given a gift, my sweet one. The gift of free will. When a soul leaves Heaven to go to Earth, it carries the light within, but it also gains the freedom to choose—to draw closer to the light or to move away from it. Every choice shapes their journey. Some choose paths that bring them into darkness, forgetting their own light. But even in the darkest night, the light within them still burns, waiting to be remembered."

The girl's lips trembled as she watched the suffering below. "But, Father," she said, "it hurts to see them like this. They look so lost, so alone. I can't just sit here. I have to do something. I have to help them."

God studied her for a long moment. "Are you sure this is what you want?" He asked. "If you go, you will leave the peace of this place. You will forget everything—who you are, where you came from, even Me. The path you are choosing is not an easy one." Her eyes, so young yet filled with ancient wisdom, met His. "I'm sure. If I can help even one soul find their way back home, it will be worth it. I can't leave them behind."

God's expression softened, a mixture of pride and sorrow. "Very well, my brave one. If this is your choice, I will honor it. But before you go, I have something for you."

The little girl leaned forward eagerly. "What is it?"

From His hand, God revealed a golden locket, its surface etched with symbols that seemed to shimmer and dance in the eternal light. He placed it gently around her neck, the chain settling close to her heart.

He placed it gently around her neck, the chain settling close to her heart.
Inside this locket," He said, "is a single seed. It is a piece of Me, planted within you. When you descend to Earth, this seed will remain with you, even when you forget everything else. In your darkest moments, when the shadows feel overwhelming and you feel lost, this seed will remind you of who you truly are."

The girl's small fingers brushed the locket, her heart swelling with an emotion she couldn't name. "How will I know? How will I remember?" God smiled, His voice like a gentle melody. "When the time is right, you will open the locket. You may think the seed is gone, but you will hear My voice, softly whispering, 'The seed has always been inside you.' It will bloom in your heart, and you will remember that you are a bearer of light, a vessel of the divine. You are not just going to Earth; you are carrying Heaven within you. Your birthright, my child, is to bring that light to others, to remind them of their own divinity, and to guide them home."

Tears sparkled in the girl's eyes, though she didn't fully understand the gravity of His words. She only knew she was ready. "I will do my best," she said, her voice steady.

God leaned close, His presence enveloping her in warmth and love. "You are loved, wholly and completely. Even when you forget, I will hold you in My embrace. You are never truly apart from Me, no matter how far you wander." The girl nodded, her determination unshaken. She stood, taking one last look at the radiant expanse of Heaven before stepping forward. As she descended, her light began to fade, her memories of this sacred moment slipping away like a dream. But the locket remained, resting against her heart, its seed quietly waiting. And so, she fell to Earth, not as a punishment but as a promise—a piece of Heaven walking among the shadows, carrying the light that could never be extinguished, destined to awaken and help others find their way back to the eternal embrace of love.

Remembrance

Remembrance

You were born a blazing star,
light woven into sacred form,
breath stolen from eternity's chest,
crafted wild, untamed, and warm.
But the world laid masks upon you,
layer upon layer, thick with dust,
buried your fire beneath its ashes,
taught you silence, called it trust.
"Shrink," they said, "become much less,
fold your wings, forget your flame.
Bite your tongue and call it kindness,
dim your light and bear no name."
But peace was never quiet chains,
nor silence where your truth should be.
It is the voice that sings unshaken,
the soul unbound, wild and free.
Do you not feel it stir within,
the ember they could not erase?
The hum of something vast, unbroken,
still singing underneath the weight?
Rise—shake the dust from your heart,
pull back the veil of their lies.
Your glory was never lost,
only waiting to be realized.
Step into the mirror and see:
you are the universe,
remembering itself.

Stand on Your Truth

Stand on Your Truth

Don't be a "kinda, maybe" soul,
A shadow shrinking, half, not whole.
Speak the fire that burns inside,
Let the raw, untamed truth collide.
Stop folding yourself to fit their mold,
Stop trading your fire for something cold.
Your truth is wild, it's sharp, it's real—
Stand on it now, let the world feel.
They'll call it rebellion; you'll call it free,
The audacity to say, "I am me."
No apologies, no playing small—
Rise up. Take it. Own it all.
Let them see the power you contain,
The storm that's risen from the pain.
This life is yours—no backing away,
Stand on your truth and lead the way.

Take Me Down Deep

Take Me Down Deep

Take me down deep,
beneath the noise,
beyond the masks I wear,
to where truth flows silently
and the soul whispers its knowing.
Strip away what is not real—
the fears, the stories,
the illusions I've carried.
Let me reach the unshakable core,
untouched by chaos,
alive with divine stillness.
In the quiet, I will remember:
I am infinite.
I am whole.
I am the pulse of creation,
free and eternal.
Take me down deep,
so I may awaken as I truly am.

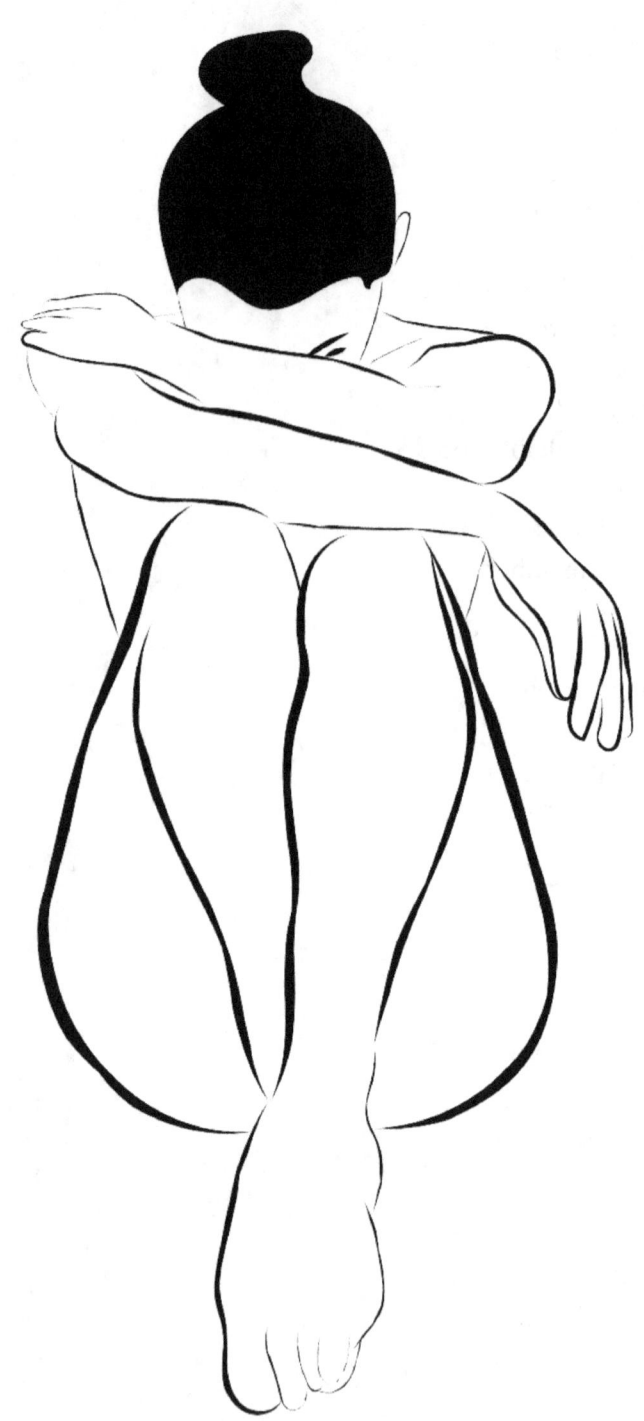

The Place Where We Hide

The Place Where We Hide

A child behind the curtain stands,
small hands pressed against his eyes.
Feet stick out, yet in his mind,
he's vanished from the seeker's sight.
"If I can't see them, they can't see me,"
he whispers soft, convinced he's free.
But the seeker moves without a doubt,
knowing well what fear shuts out.
We clutch the veil, pretend, disguise,
press our palms to guarded eyes,
as if the heavens could be blind,
as if love retreats from where we hide.
No shadow swallows what is seen,
no silence keeps us out of view.
Even in our deepest hiding,
heaven has its eyes on you.
For we do not slip beyond its reach,
nor drift where love won't dare pursue.
The only place we go unseen—
is from the truth we know is true.

Beneath the Silence

Beneath the Silence

Beneath the silence,
a soft voice speaks,
like wind over water,
sending ripples across the stillness.
It does not shout,
for truth is never loud.
It hums behind the mind's chatter,
a quiet call to return.
It is the whisper of your essence,
unbroken, unyielding,
longing to be felt,
to expand and
reveal
what has always been.
In the silence,
I hear it—
gentle but unwavering,
a guide back to myself.

Reveal You

Reveal You

You were not sent here to shatter under the weight,
To crumble beneath the storms that came too late.
No, the cracks in your armor were carved to expose,
The raw, untamed power your spirit still holds.
Every betrayal, every scarred night,
Was the hammer and chisel sculpting your light.
Not wounds, but windows to the truth you hide,
The unbroken core you've kept inside.
The world didn't crush you—it burned you clean,
A wildfire consuming what might have been.
Ashes fall, but they feed the ground,
So your roots grow deeper, unbound, unbound.
Not abandoned, but tempered—polished by cost.
Those tears you thought were the end of the line
Were rivers carving the shape of the divine.
Stand naked in the mirror, stripped to the bone,
See yourself clearer, raw and alone.
You are not the ruins, you're the rising flame,
The proof that survival is more than a game.
No victim here, no martyr crowned,
You are the roar that shakes the ground.
This world tested you, not to see you fall—
But to reveal you, above it all.
Now soar with the fury of a soul laid bare,
Not fragile, but fearless, alive and aware.
This is the truth they don't want you to see—
Your hardships didn't break you; they set you free.

The Tender Nudge of Truth

The Tender Nudge of Truth

It comes not as a roar,
but as a breath—
soft, insistent,
unfolding in the quiet.
The tender nudge of truth
does not demand;
it invites,
gentle as dawn
spilling across a darkened room.
You've felt it before,
a stirring beneath the noise,
a faint pull toward what you know
but cannot name.
It is not cruel,
though it may undo you.
It does not wound,
though it may strip you bare.
For truth is a mirror,
and to see yourself
is to see all.
It moves through you
like wind shaping stone—
steady, deliberate, patient.
It does not rush;
it waits for your heart
to soften,
to yield,
to say yes.
And when you do,
it blooms,
not as fire,
but as light—
a quiet radiance,
a steady knowing,
that was yours
all along.

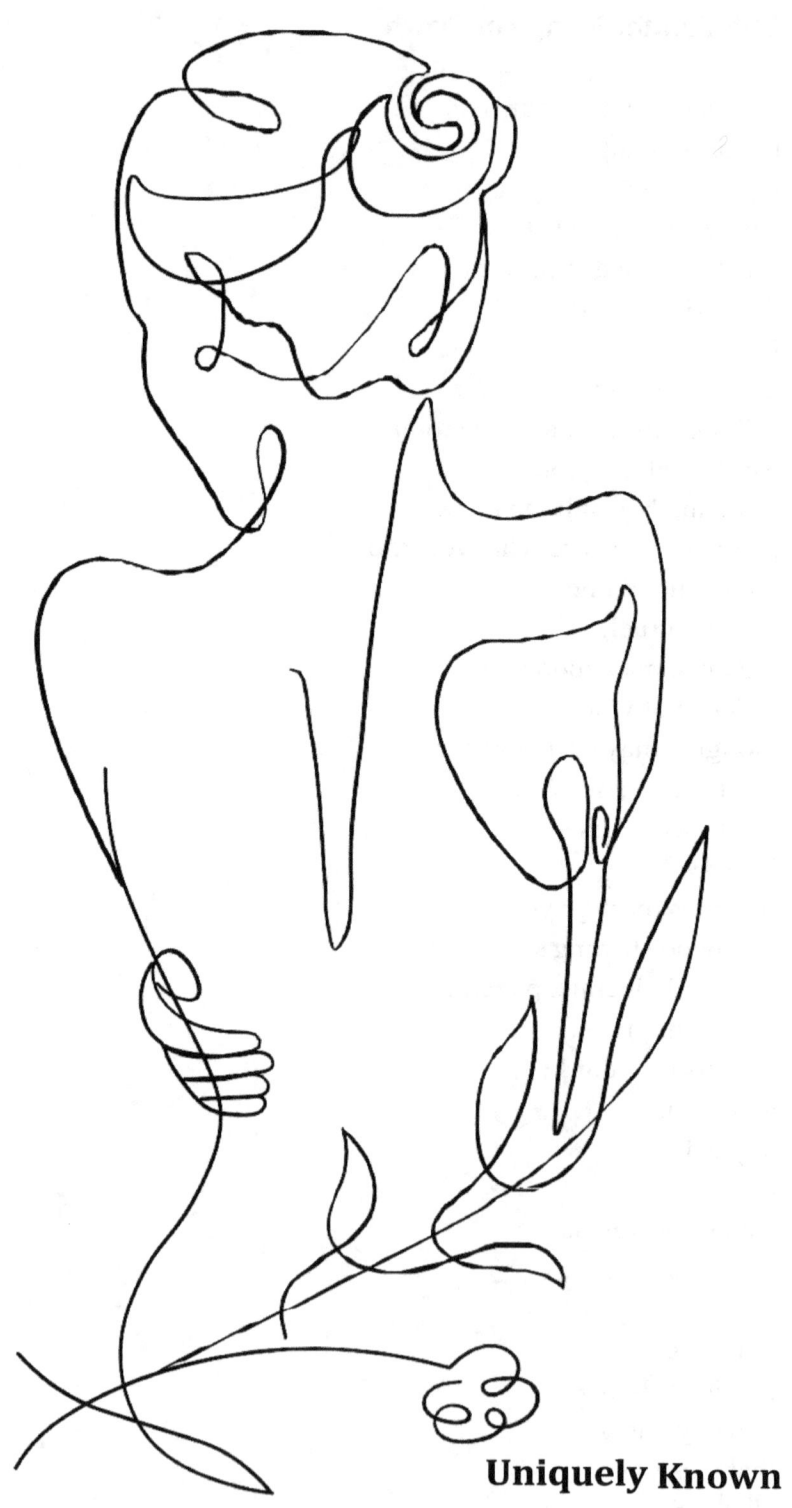

Uniquely Known

Uniquely Known

You are not special.
Not above, not below—
not set apart in a gilded frame
or crowned by the weight of imagined glory.
Let this truth unmake you.
Let it humble your heart
as you fall to your knees,
stripped bare of the need to be more.
"What is special about me?"
You cry into the
void. The answer
comes, sharp as a
blade: "Nothing."
And in the nothing,
you weep.
For the pedestal crumbles,
the illusion shatters,
and the self you thought you were,
falls away.
But then—
a voice rises from the depths,
soft as the breath of dawn,
vast as eternity's embrace:
"You are uniquely known."
Not by name,
but by essence,
by the song only you can sing
within the great symphony of being.
The whole of life has marked you
into its memory,
held you in its deepest reverence,
for only you
can be what you are.
There is no replacement,

no mirror, no reverberation.
The universe knows your every thread,
woven deliberately
into the infinite tapestry of existence.
A table has been prepared for you—
not because you are greater,
but because you are here.
The feast is life itself,
and it waits for no one else.
Take your place,
not in arrogance,
but in awe.
You are not special.
You are something far greater:
a truth so singular,
so wholly irreplaceable,
that all of creation bows
to your being.

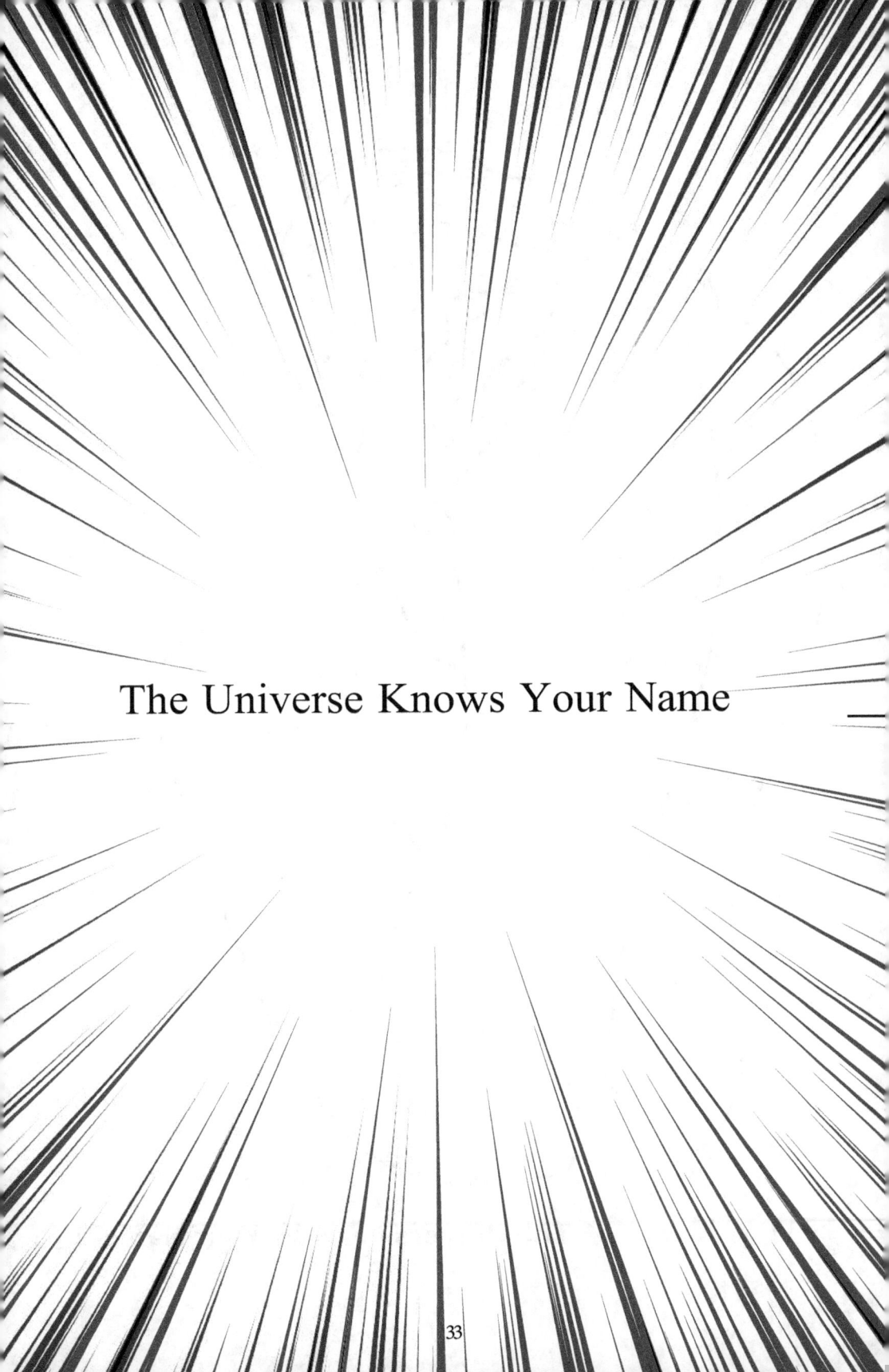

The Universe Knows Your Name

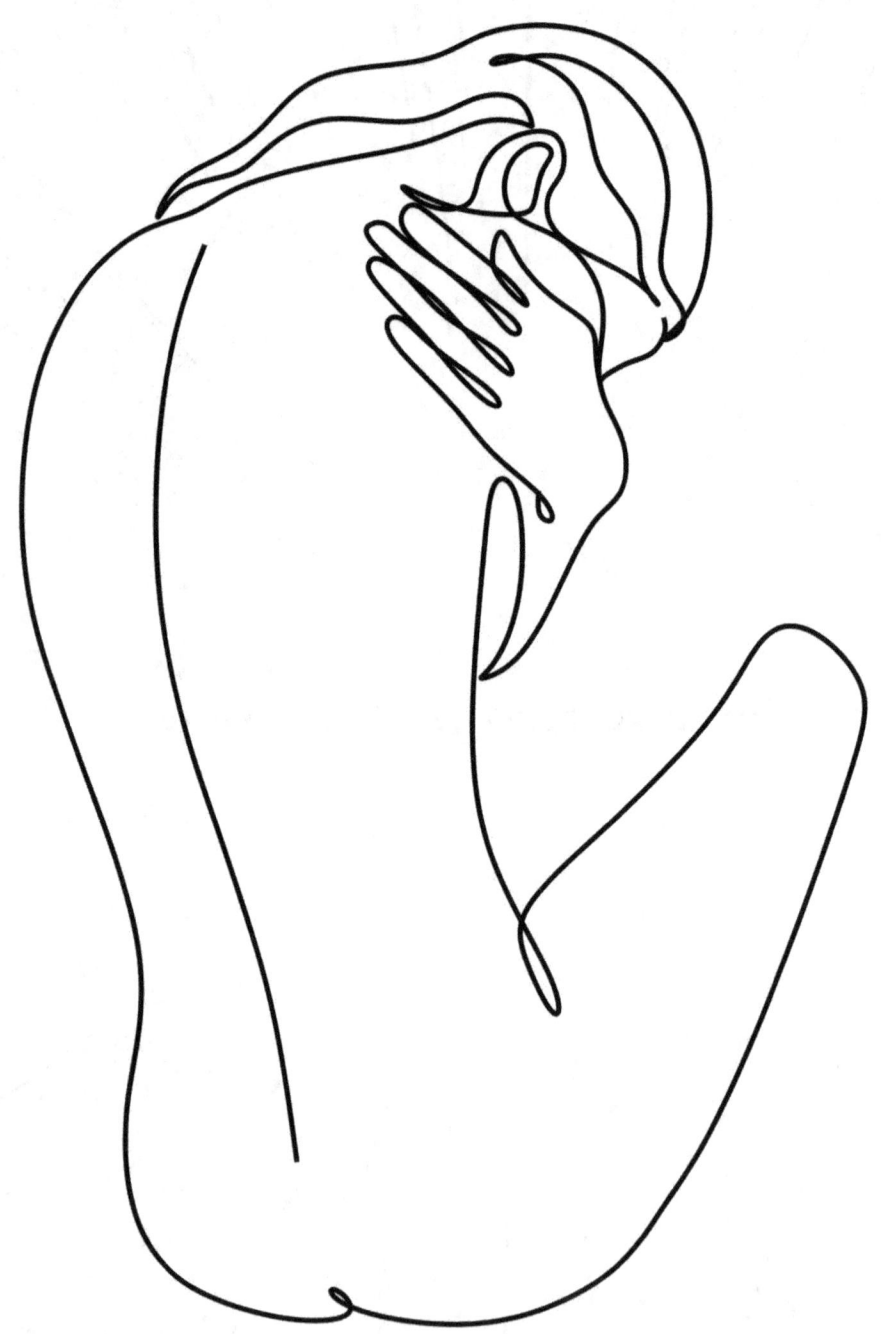

The Universe Knows Your Name

The Universe Knows Your Name

You are not lost,
though the world may tell you so.
Not unseen,
though the shadows may try to hide you.
The stars have carved your essence
into the fabric of all that is—
a light that cannot dim,
a presence that cannot fade.
The universe knows your name.
It was whispered in the birth of the cosmos,
infused into the rhythm of the tides,
sung by the winds that dance
across the vast and endless sky.
Every breath you take
is answered by its ripple,
a quiet assurance
that you belong.
You are woven into its vastness,
a thread of infinite design,
unbreakable, irreplaceable, whole.
Feel its pull in the stillness,
its embrace in the rising sun.
You are not forgotten,
for how could the infinite forget
the very heart of its creation?
The universe knows your name.
And in the knowing,
you are found.

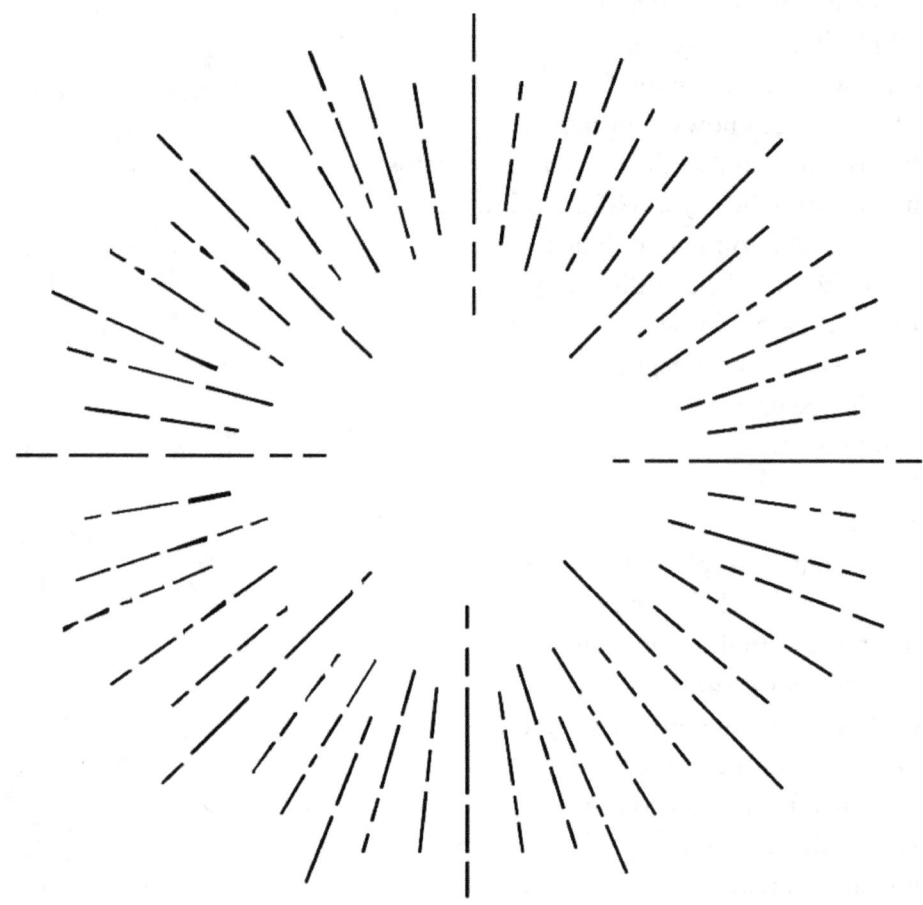

Happiness

Happiness

Happiness is not a fleeting breath,
nor a moment caught in time.
It is the stillness between worlds,
the quiet rhythm of the eternal.
It does not bloom from the outer,
from the shifting sands of circumstance.
It is the flame that burns within,
undisturbed by the winds of life.
Happiness is the knowing
that all things are connected—
that you are the spark of the divine,
and all of creation flows through you.
It is the joy of being whole,
not in the becoming,
but in the remembering
of your true nature.
In the vastness of the cosmos,
happiness is the song sung by the stars,
the peace in the pulse of the earth,
the love that moves through every breath.
To seek it outside
is to miss the truth within—
for happiness is not a destination,
but the essence of who you are.

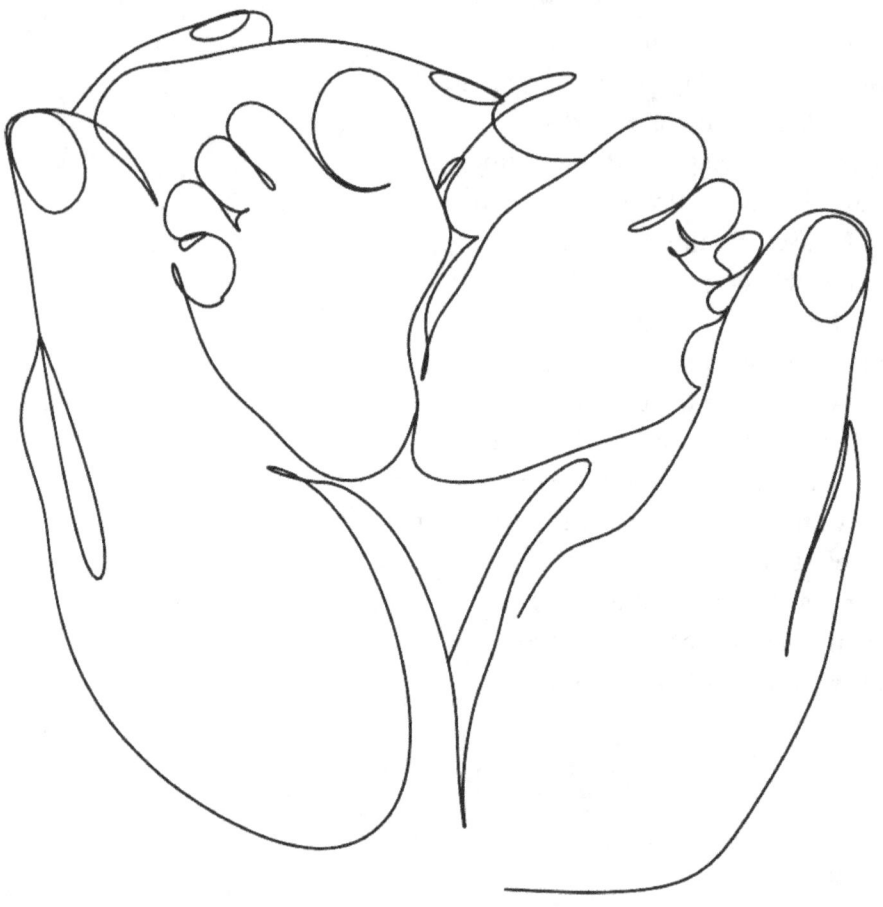

The Mirror of Creation

The Mirror of Creation

The mirror of creation reflects you
as a mother sees her child for the first time—
a being of pure perfection,
crafted in love's tender hands.
Her heart expands beyond limits,
overflowing with a love so boundless
it radiates through eternity.
It is as a father feels
when he cradles his newborn,
his hands trembling with awe,
his soul humbled by the sacred weight of life.
In that moment,
he knows he is closer to the divine
than ever before,
for the divine reveals itself
in the fragile wonder
resting in his arms.
This is how creation knows you—
not as broken,
not as lost,
but as the miracle you are.
Every breath you take
is cherished,
every part of your being
wrapped in a love so pure,
it transcends all understanding.
The mirror of creation reflects
the way life celebrates itself—
with awe,
with joy,
with the knowing
that you are love made manifest.

Finding Freedom

Finding Freedom

Freedom is not a distant dream,
not a place you'll find tomorrow,
but the truth you hold within,
the power that lies in your own hands.
It is the knowing that the world
does not shape you,
but you shape the world—
that every thought you think
is a seed planted in the soil of your soul.
What you believe becomes your reality,
the universe bends to the power of your belief.
What you assume to be true
becomes your world—
and in that truth,
your freedom is found.
You are not anchored by circumstance,
not limited by what has been.
In the depth of your heart,
you hold the key to the life you seek—
unlock it with your thoughts,
set your soul free.
To claim what is yours
is to declare your worth,
that abundance is yours,
that peace is yours,
that love is yours.
In the freedom of your own belief,
you become the creator of your existence,
the architect of your future,
the master of your own liberation.
What you believe is what you become.
And so, you elevate.

Diamond in the Rough

Diamond in the Rough

A diamond begins as nothing more
than a fragment buried in the dark—
coal pressed and shaped
by forces unseen,
by the weight of the earth,
and the fire of transformation.
It does not resist the pressure,
nor curse the heat;
it knows that what seems like destruction
is the path to its becoming.
The process is not punishment
but refinement,
a divine alchemy
turning the ordinary into the eternal.
So too are you shaped,
by trials that seem unyielding,
by moments that press you into yourself,
breaking illusions,
revealing the brilliance within.
You are not lost in the rough;
you are being polished by life itself,
chiseled by the unseen hand of creation,
your edges softened,
your light revealed.
When the pressure ceases,
when the fire subsides,
you will know the truth:
You were always a diamond.
The rough was simply the stage
for your magnificence to emerge.

Wings of Becoming

Wings of Becoming

From the cocoon of stillness, I emerge,
Bound in silence, yet alive with yearning,
The threads of limitation tightly wound,
Yet within, a quiet knowing is burning.
The caterpillar dreams not of wings,
Yet the code of flight is sown inside,
A map inscribed by the eternal Source,
Waiting for the moment to collide.
The chrysalis becomes a sacred tomb,
A place where the old dissolves away,
No turning back, no clinging to form—
Only surrender to the alchemy of decay.
The butterfly rises, unbound, renewed,
Its wings, a tapestry of infinite grace,
Reflect the freedom we hold inside,
A testament to life's sacred embrace.
For we, too, are born to dissolve and ascend,
To shed the husk of the known and confined,
And embrace the truth written in our soul—
We are creation, wholly aligned.

Forgotten Magnificence

Forgotten Magnificence

You stand at the edge of eternity,
a spark of the divine veiled in form,
forgetting that you are the very pulse of creation—
the breath of stars,
the song of the universe.
You have wandered through lifetimes,
wearing the masks of the world,
shaped by its illusions,
its rules, its boundaries—
but deep within,
beneath the layers of dust and time,
there is a truth that cannot be hidden.
You are magnificence incarnate,
a reflection of the infinite.
The universe itself whispers your name,
reminding you of the grandeur that lies within.
You have forgotten,
but only for a moment,
for the seed of your highest self
rests within your heart—
an eternal flame,
waiting to be remembered.
In the silence of your soul,
you are whole,
you are boundless,
you are the embodiment of pure potential.
No force in the cosmos
can diminish the light that you are.
You are not separate from divinity,
you are its most sacred expression—
woven into the canvas of the divine,
part of the cosmic dance
that transcends all space and time.

You are the answer you seek.
You are the divine within the flesh,
the eternal made manifest,
the magnificence of the universe
expressed in human form.
Know this,
and remember who you are—
for the magnificence of your being
is waiting to be awakened,
to shine through the veil,
to emerge in the fullness of your
truth. And when you remember,
the world will know,
for you are the mirror of creation itself,
the divine reflected in human form.

I am the keeper of a sacred legacy, born from love and divinity.

Journey to the Blossoming Rose

Journey to the Blossoming Rose

The seed did not question the darkness,
nor did it curse the weight of the earth above.
It simply knew—deep in the marrow of its being—
that it was meant for more than the silence of soil.
With time, the first sprout pressed against the unknown,
stretching toward a sun it had never seen,
breaking through the soil not in rebellion,
but in trust.
Yet the path was never soft,
for the stem bore thorns—
sharp reminders of pain,
lessons carved in crimson,
proof that growth demands its price.
Each thorn a trial, a wound, a quiet call,
each one asking:
"Will you turn back?"
"Will you fold beneath the weight?"
"Will you mistake the pain for punishment?"
But the rose does not fear its own becoming.
It does not question the necessity of its thorns.
It climbs, it reaches, it endures—
for it knows that beyond the trials,
beyond the piercing ache of transformation,
awaits the bloom.
And when the moment of unfolding arrives,
it is not hesitant, nor ashamed.
The petals unfurl in soft defiance,
offering their fragrance without condition,
their beauty without apology,
their existence without restraint.
For the rose has always known:
The climb was never in vain.

The wounds were never the end.
Every thorn was simply the hand of the Divine,
guiding it closer—
not just to the sun,
but to itself.
And so, it stands,
radiant in its full becoming,
a testament to all who doubt their own path—
that the journey, no matter how treacherous,
was always meant to lead you home.

I trust the timing of my unfolding.

Arriving Is the Inevitable

Arriving Is the Inevitable

You can stall, you can wander,
take the long road, take the detour,
wrap yourself in doubt like an old, tattered coat—
but destiny? She waits for no one.
The universe grins, leaning back with knowing,
watching you dance around what's already yours.
You pretend you don't hear the call,
but even silence carries your name.
Go ahead, hesitate.
Second-guess your greatness, shrink if you must.
But the river still flows,
the stars still burn,
and time still pulls you toward the truth—
arriving is the inevitable.
You were never meant to stay lost.
The breadcrumbs were always there,
glowing in the dark like embers of home.
Each misstep, a perfect step,
each fall, a rise in disguise.
The Divine laughs—not at you, but with you,
for it knows what you will soon remember:
There is no other ending,
no alternate fate,
only you—stepping into what was always meant to be.
So quit resisting, quit pretending,
surrender to the rhythm already humming in your bones.
You are not finding the path—
you are the path.
And it has only one destination:
Home.

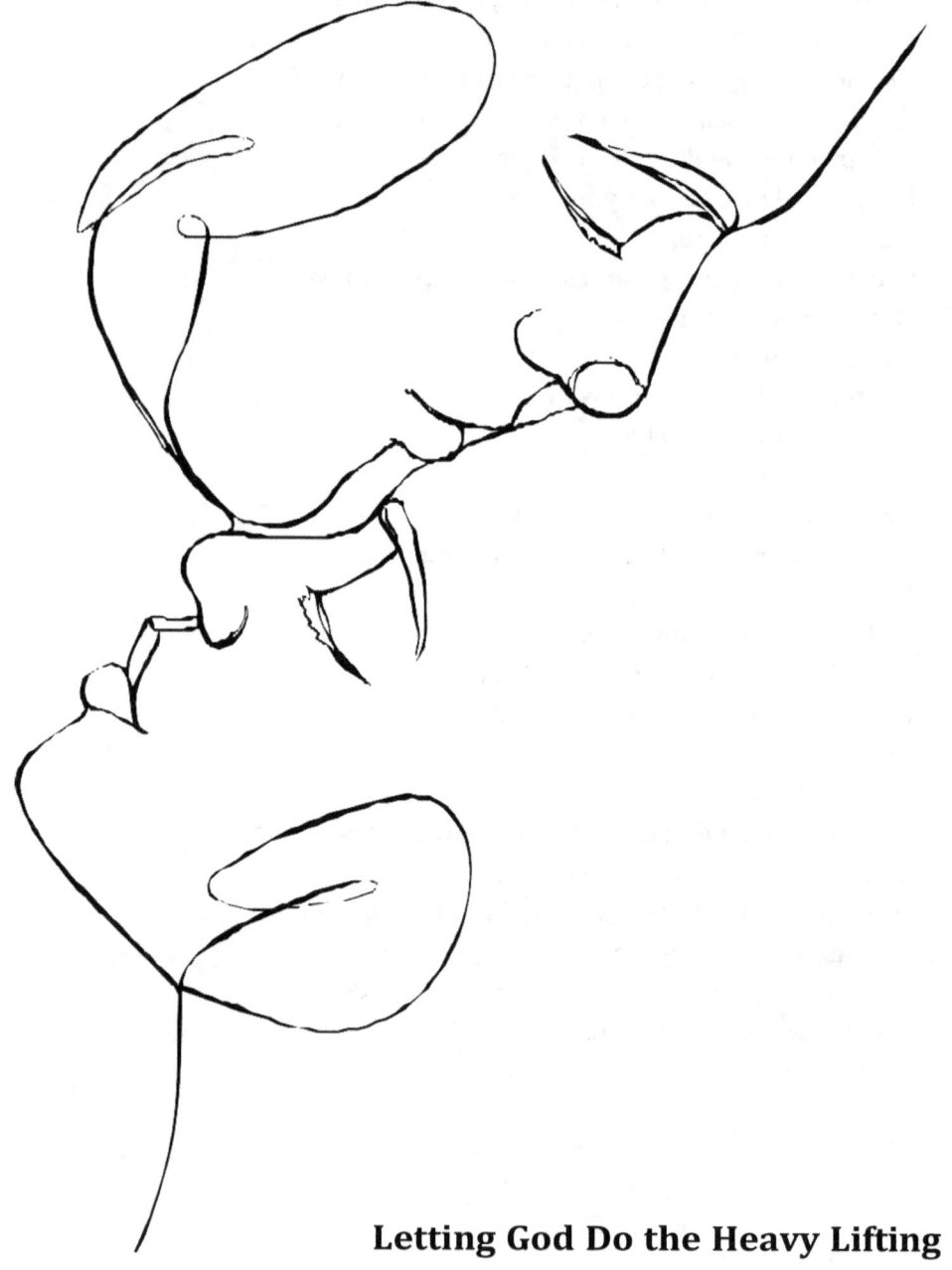

Letting God Do the Heavy Lifting

Letting God Do the Heavy Lifting

Release the weight you were never meant to carry,
the burdens that bend your spirit low.
The universe moves with ease,
its rhythm unforced,
its flow unbroken—
so why must you labor against the tide?
Let go.
Trust the unseen hands
that weave your path with care,
the wisdom far greater than your grasp.
In surrender,
there is strength.
In stillness,
there is movement.
To let God do the heavy lifting
is not to abandon the work
but to align with the source—
where effort becomes grace,
and struggle dissolves into peace.
Lay it down.
Let the divine carry what you cannot,
and find the freedom
that was always yours to claim.

I Didn't Come Here to Be Who You Wanted Me to Be

I Didn't Come Here to Be Who You Wanted Me to Be

I did not come here to fit within your lines,
To shrink myself so your comfort shines.
I was not born to be palatable, small,
To twist my truth so you stand tall.
I did not come here to dim my light,
To apologize for my fire burning bright.
I am not a whisper, I am the roar,
Not a locked window, but an open door.
I did not come here seeking your grace,
To soften my edges or mask my face.
I was shaped by storms, carved by sea,
A force of nature, wild and free.
I did not come here to make you at ease,
To swallow my truth or bend my knees.
I was woven from stars, meant to expand,
Not to be tamed by another's hand.
I did not come here to be less than whole,
To quiet my fire, to barter my soul.
I stand in my essence, no "sorry" to give,
I came here to be me—fully, and live.

Surrender Is Grace in Action

Surrender Is Grace in Action

Surrender is not bending to loss;
it is the quiet choice to remember truth.
It is the undoing of fear,
the soft release of all illusions
that veil the light within.
In surrender, there is no sacrifice,
only freedom.
For what can be lost
but chains we forged in error?
What can be gained
but the peace of knowing
we were never bound?
Grace moves where resistance ends,
a current of love
that lifts all burdens,
a quiet voice that whispers:
You are held.
Through surrender, the miracle unfolds—
not as an outside force,
but as the unveiling of what always was.
The light in you,
unchanged,
unshaken,
is waiting to shine.
When you release the need to fight,
to control,
to understand every step,
you align with the divine rhythm
that knows the way home.
Surrender is grace in action—
a sacred remembering
that you are already free.

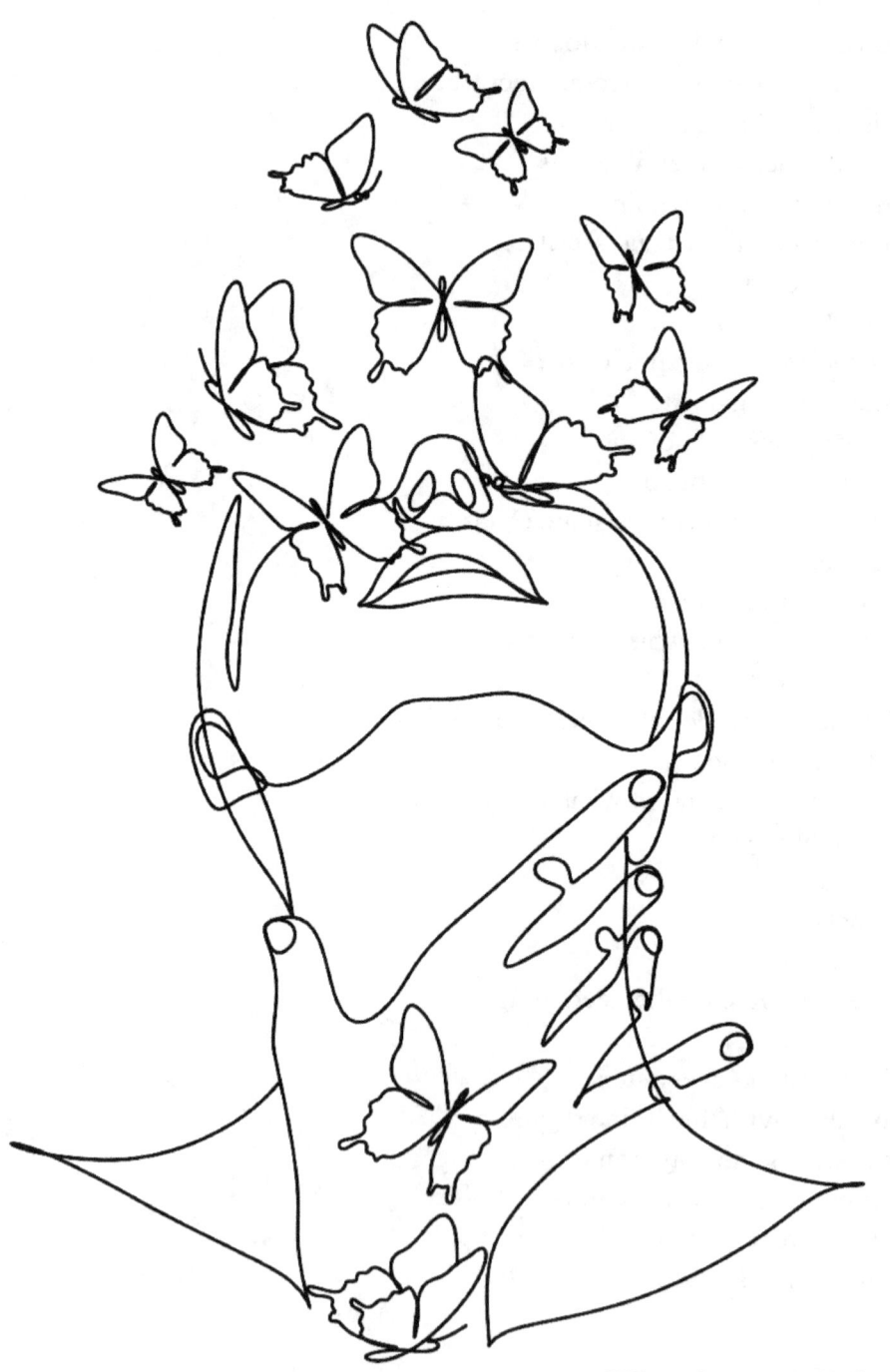

The Guru Within

The Guru Within

In the stillness of your being,
A quiet presence waits,
Not distant, but woven into the tapestry
Of all that you are.
It does not shout;
It speaks in gentle currents—
The pull of intuition,
The flicker of truth that lights
The darkest corners of doubt.
This is the wisdom you have sought,
Not in the words of others
But in the boundless expanse
Of your own soul.
The guru within is no stranger;
It is the essence of you,
The eternal witness,
Holding the map to your freedom.
Each step inward peels away the veil,
Each moment of surrender reveals the path.
You are not apart from divinity;
You are its expression,
Its light,
Its song.
The world may call you outward,
But the truth waits within—
Whole, radiant,
And endlessly alive.

I Am the Safe Space to Fall in Love with Myself

I Am the Safe Space to Fall in Love with Myself

Within me, there is a sanctuary,
A haven untouched by judgment,
Where every shadow is embraced
And every wound cradled with tenderness.
Here, I lay down the armor
Worn from battles against myself.
Here, I rest in the arms of acceptance,
Unraveling the lies I once believed.
I am the soft ground beneath my own feet,
The steady rhythm that calms my storms,
The quiet voice that whispers,
"You are enough—just as you are."
In this sacred space within,
I meet my reflection anew,
Not with harsh eyes or heavy hands,
But with a love that feels like coming home.
I am my own shelter,
The gentle place where my heart can land.
And in this safe space,
I fall in love with all that I am.

There Will Never Be Another You

There Will Never Be Another You

No hands have ever shaped another
with the symmetry of your soul,
no breath has stirred the stars
to form a being quite like you.
You are the only reflection of your kind,
the only flame burning in your hue—
a note in the great celestial song
that no other voice can sing.
Do you see it?
How the lines of your palms
are written like scripture,
how your scars are constellations
marking the journey only you have walked.
There will never be another you.
No one will ever laugh with your rhythm,
or carry the precise weight of your dreams.
No other feet will dance in your footsteps,
or touch the world in the way you do.
And so, do not shrink to fit the mold,
do not carve yourself into another's silhouette.
The world is waiting for what only you can bring,
for the fire that only you can light.
Stand tall in the temple of your being.
Let your presence be an offering,
a testament to the miracle of existence—
because once you are gone,
the universe will never again
know your name in the same way.

The Sacred Song of Return

The Sacred Song of Return

A melody stirs within, ancient and deep,
A call that hums through the chambers of sleep.
Not a sound the ears can hold or confine,
But a hymn of the soul, eternal, divine.
The body, a temple, both humble and vast,
Holds the secrets of future and whispers of past.
Each cell a star, each breath a prayer,
Infinity murmurs, "I am everywhere."
The spine, a pillar of light untold,
Carries the song as the stories unfold.
Hidden pathways awaken in time,
Aligning the self to the infinite rhyme.
Through the dance of the breath, the stillness of thought,
The soul remembers the truths it once sought.
It sings to the stars, it bows to the earth,
It honors the body, the cradle of rebirth.
For to journey within is to journey back home,
To the Source from which all creation has grown.
In the sacred temple, the infinite waits,
Opening the door to love's boundless gates.
And so, let the song rise, let it reclaim,
The sacred, the infinite, within your name.
For the body and soul, a holy embrace,
Return to the infinity, your eternal space.

The Unblemished Soul

The Unblemished Soul

You cannot wound what is untouched by time,
The spark eternal, pure, and sublime.
No scar can taint, no shadow stain,
The essence of you that remains untamed.
The ego shatters, fractured and small,
A house of mirrors destined to fall.
It clings to wounds, claiming offense,
Demanding it all, in hollow defense.
Who are you, beneath the masks you wear?
Not the name, not the story, not the despair.
Strip it all away—let it all burn,
And to the unbroken, you will return.
But the soul watches, silent and still,
Untouched by chaos, unmoved by will.
It does not falter, it does not fear—
Whispering softly, "You were never here."
This self cannot be offended or bruised,
For it does not cling, it cannot refuse.
In the silence of being, you find your goal—
The sacred knowing of your unblemished soul.
It knows no victim, no victor, no shame,
It stands beyond the fleeting game.
Dare to release who you think you are,
Let the ego dissolve like a dying star.
Step into the vastness, the boundless whole,
And meet the truth—your unblemished soul.

Forged in Fire

Forged in Fire

There is a fire that does not burn,
A sacred blaze where all may turn.
Its flames do not destroy but refine,
An altar of truth, both human and divine.
Step into this furnace, trembling yet whole,
Let it consume the illusions of your soul.
The masks you've worn, the lies you've told,
All crumble like ash, releasing their hold.
This fire is not of punishment or pain,
But a cleansing light where love remains.
It burns through the layers of fear and disguise,
Revealing the Self that never dies.
Here, the ego dissolves, fragile and thin,
And the voice of the sacred rises within.
It whispers not of what you've lost,
But of the truth reclaimed at any cost.
In the fire's heart, the past unwinds,
Its chains unshackle the infinite mind.
The body, a vessel, purified and clear,
Holds the essence of what's always been near.
From this forging, a being renewed,
Whole and radiant, divinely imbued.
No longer bound by the weight of the past,
You are the light, eternal and vast.
Step forward now, with vision restored,
A bearer of peace, infinite and adored.
For in the sacred fire, you've come to see—
The soul is eternal, unbound, and free.

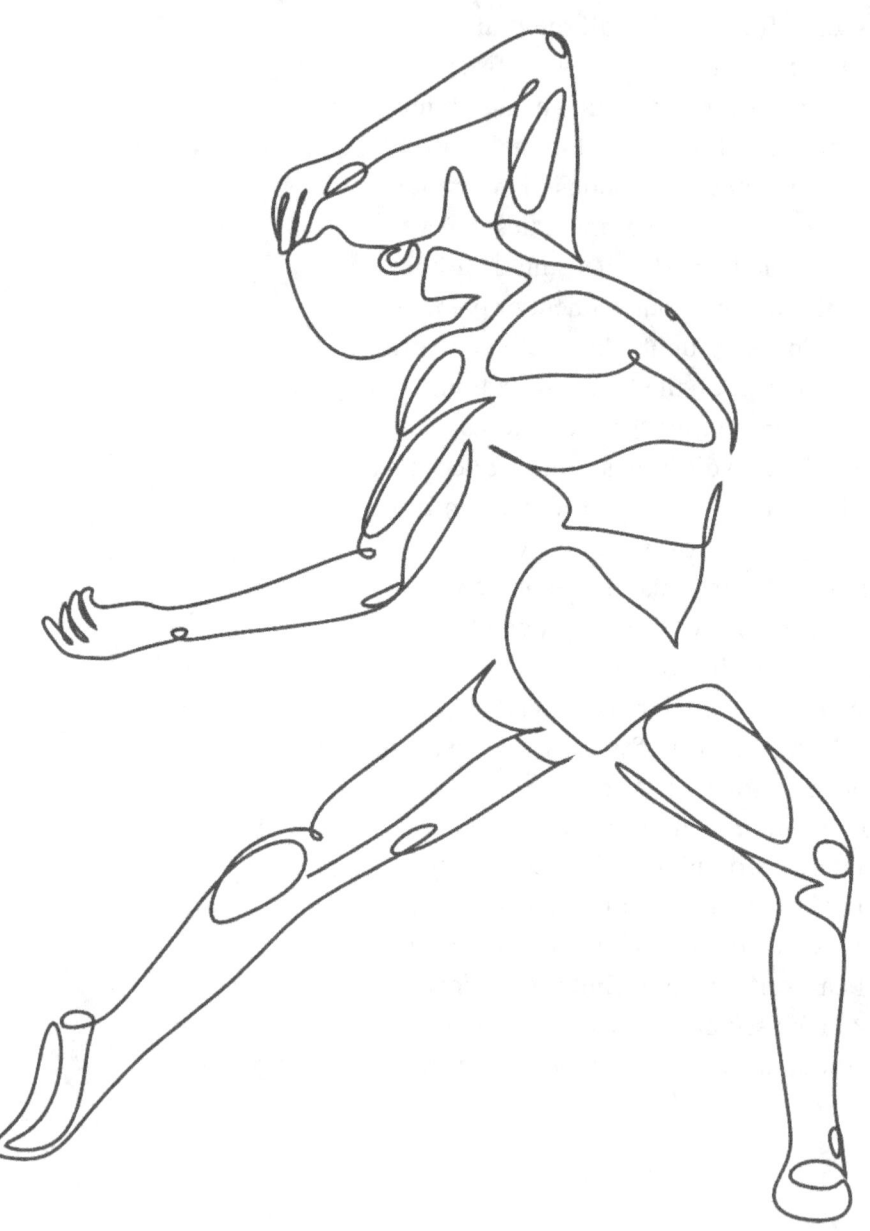

No Longer Dancing in the Den of Thieves

No Longer Dancing in the Den of Thieves

I once danced among the shadows,
In the den of thieves who spoke in silken lies.
They held out empty promises,
Gold-painted chains disguised as freedom.
They fed on my light,
Called it theirs, then left me hollow,
Scattering pearls before their unclean feet.
"Do not cast your pearls before swine,"
The ancient words whispered in my soul,
Yet I ignored the wisdom,
Believing love could change the unchangeable,
Believing grace could awaken hearts sealed shut.
But a soul unwilling to face its own reflection
Will never rise to meet the light,
And love cannot bloom in a barren field.
So I stood still,
The music of the thieves fading to silence,
Their clamor no longer drowning my truth.
The chains I thought were bonds of love
Shattered as I stepped into the light.
The den could no longer contain me,
For my spirit was never meant to bow to thieves.
I turned my gaze to higher ground,
Where the air is clean,
And the soul finds its rightful rest.
There, I no longer offer my jewels
To those who cannot see their worth.
I save them for hands that honor,
For hearts that understand their sacred glow.
The den of thieves still calls,
But I do not answer.
My dance now belongs to the heavens,
Where truth reigns,
Where love is not stolen, but freely given.
I am no longer a captive to shadows.

Reclaiming My Throne

Reclaiming My Throne

I have walked through fire and silence,
through the ruins of who I was told to be.
I have knelt in the dust of forgotten dreams,
believing the world had stolen my name.
But no more.
I gather the scattered pieces,
the fragments of a soul once dimmed.
I dust off the weight of unspoken truths
and step into the light of my own becoming.
No longer will I bow to borrowed narratives,
to the voices that tried to tame my wild.
I was never meant to shrink or fold—
I was always meant to rise.
I ascend the staircase carved in stars,
each step a reclamation of what is mine.
Power not taken, but remembered,
not stolen, but restored.
I crown myself in sovereignty,
wrapped in the gold of my own knowing.
No permission, no apology—
only the quiet certainty of a throne reclaimed.

Close to the Bone

Close to the Bone

When you pray, do not skim the surface,
do not offer words like drifting leaves,
light enough to dance on the wind
and too weak to take root in the soil.
Pray close to the bone—
where the marrow hums with ancient knowing,
where the fire of longing burns
too deep to be spoken in whispers.
Let your words crack open the hollow places,
let them press against your ribs,
let them sink like rain into parched earth
until they tremble in the roots of your being.
Do not pray as one asking permission,
but as one reclaiming their birthright.
Do not kneel in fear, but in fierce remembrance—
for the hands you lift have always been holy.
Pray not to the sky alone,
but to the breath within your lungs,
to the blood that carries the old songs,
to the silence between heartbeats
where the Divine has always waited.
And when you rise,
do not wait for a sign carved in stone—
for the answer is already written
in the marrow of your soul.

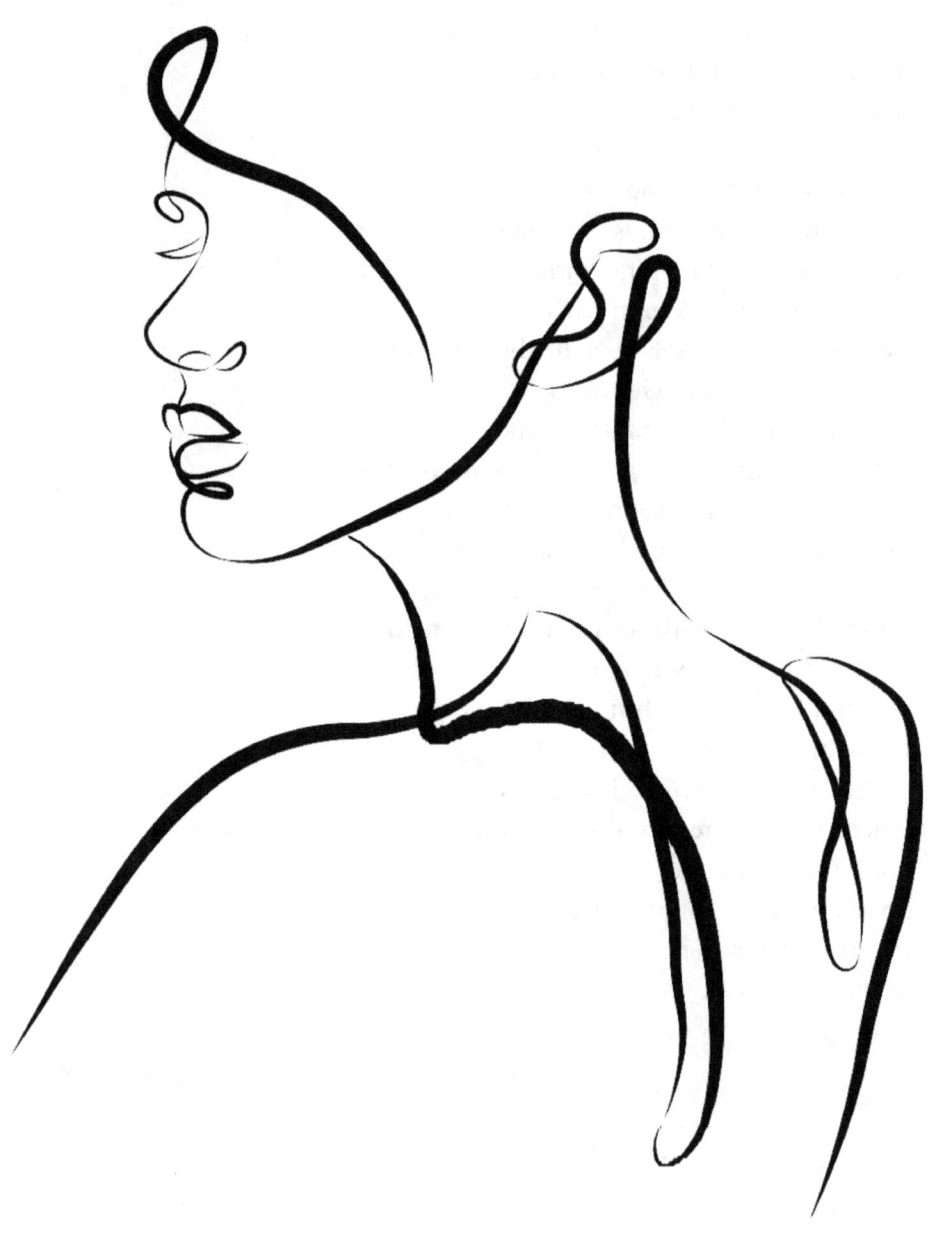

I Am Steady

I Am Steady

I am steady, unshaken, whole,
The quiet strength of an anchored soul.
Through storms that howl and shadows creep,
I stand in truth, my peace runs deep.
No fear can sway, no doubt can bind,
I am the calm the world can't find.
Rooted in love, in light I stay,
Steady and sure, come what may.

Stepping Into Your Great

Stepping Into Your Great

Step like the ground was built for you,
like the sun rises just to watch you move.
Own the space, breathe it in—
this world was never meant to make you small.
Stepping into your great,
even when doubt tugs at your sleeve,
even when fear mutters "not yet,"
even when the past begs you to turn back.
You were not sent here to hesitate,
to tiptoe around your own power.
You were made to walk boldly,
to leave footprints soaked in purpose.
Let the unsure moments shape you,
let the stumbles teach you rhythm.
Greatness is not in perfection—
it's in the getting up, the moving forward,
the knowing that even a slow step is still a step.
So keep going.
Keep rising.
Keep stepping into the vastness of who you are.

My Abundance Flows to Me

My Abundance Flows to Me

Like rivers rushing to the sea,
My abundance flows endlessly.
Through every breath, through every space,
I'm met with wealth, a boundless grace.
No strain, no fear, no need to chase,
It finds me here, in perfect place.
Aligned with love, I let it be—
My abundance flows to me.

God Made No Mistake on You

God Made No Mistake on You

You were spoken into existence with purpose,
woven with hands that do not falter.
Every curve of your soul, every fiber of your being,
was sculpted to walk a path only you can tread.
Not a thread out of place, not a breath undesigned—
your laughter, your tears, your wild, unyielding heart
were not accidents, nor flaws to be erased,
but the perfect tools for the journey you were born to take.
The texture of your voice, the depth of your eyes,
the way your spirit moves through this world—
all of it, divinely measured, intentionally placed,
crafted to fit the calling that belongs to you alone.
Do not silence your spirit.
Do not fold yourself into smaller spaces.
Do not wish away the very parts of you
that were made to shine in ways no one else can.
For even your scars are sacred inscriptions,
markings of a life unfolding exactly as it should.
The wisdom in your steps, the fire in your voice,
the quiet strength you carry—none of it is by chance.
You are not separate from the divine,
for the breath of God moves through you.
You are a spark of the infinite, a note in love's eternal song,
a vessel of light made whole in your becoming.
Stand in the fullness of who you are,
for heaven's hands do not tremble,
and they did not tremble when they made you.

Let Everything in Life Inspire You

Let Everything in Life Inspire You

Let the morning sun wrap you in gold,
A reminder that each day is yours to unfold.
Let the rain cleanse more than the ground,
Washing away doubts where dreams are found.
Let the wind hum its sacred song,
Guiding you forward, steady and strong.
Let the mountains remind you to stand tall,
That even in struggle, you transcend it all.
Let your heartbreak carve wisdom deep,
For even in sorrow, love still speaks.
Let laughter ring like a hymn in your chest,
A rhythm of joy that life knows best.
Let the stars teach you how to believe,
That nothing is distant if you dare to reach.
Let silence hold you in its embrace,
For even in stillness, life leaves a trace.
But more than this—be the inspiration you seek,
A living flame, bold and unique.
Walk as a light, let your presence ignite,
A world that is waiting to shine in your sight.
Let everything in life inspire you,
Every action, both big and small.
For when you live as a spark in the dark,
You remind the world—it was made to stand tall.

God Sees What You Don't

God Sees What You Don't

You curse the closed door,
the road that crumbled beneath your feet,
the love that slipped through your hands like sand,
but what if the loss was the mercy?
What if the delay was the protection?
You rage at the silence,
the waiting that stretches beyond reason,
but God is moving in ways unseen,
aligning, shifting, weaving threads
into something far greater than you imagined.
You see the storm—
God sees the clearing.
You see the setback—
God sees the redirection.
You see the end—
God sees the beginning you are not yet ready for.
Divine timing is not rushed,
it does not answer to your impatience,
nor does it bow to your fears.
It unfolds in perfect rhythm,
not a second too early, not a moment too late.
So trust the unseen hands at work.
Trust the doors that do not open.
Trust the detours that lead you elsewhere.
One day, you will understand why things had to unfold this way.
And when that day comes,
you will look back and whisper,
"God, now I see."

I Dance with the Heartbeat of Creation

I Dance with the Heartbeat of Creation

I dance with the heartbeat of creation.
God knows my soul's song—
intimately, wholeheartedly.
I weave my body like a soft gust of wind,
rippling over a tall blade of grass,
touching the voice of my innocence's call.
In the rhythm of this sacred dance,
I find the place perfectly held just for me,
where my unblemished soul opens its knowing,
and finds its home in the center of my being.
I dance with the heartbeat of creation.
In doing so, I become the song
I have been dreaming about.

You Never Get the Same Moment Twice

You Never Get the Same Moment Twice

No river ever flows the same,
No breath returns once it leaves your name.
The hands of time refuse to rewind,
For each moment is a gift, uniquely designed.
The sunrise today is not yesterday's gold,
The wind that brushes your face won't be retold.
Every word, every glance, every fleeting embrace,
Exists only once—then vanishes without a trace.
You will never stand in this now again,
Never touch this air, never walk this bend.
Each second dissolves like a murmured prayer,
A sacred pulse, fragile and rare.
Life does not loop, it does not repeat,
It only offers new ground beneath your feet.
It asks not where you've been or what you regret,
But how you will choose in the moment that's left.
So love like it's the first and the last,
Hold nothing back, let go of the past.
See with new eyes, stand open, aware—
For now is the only place life meets you there.
You never get the same moment twice,
No remnants remain, no past reprise.
Only the now, the infinite thread,
Where eternity speaks and the soul is fed.

Worth Your Salt

Worth Your Salt

You are worth your salt,
Born of stardust and ocean tides,
A creation of the heavens,
Where eternity and earth collide.
Each grain of who you are
Carries the memory of the sea,
A whisper from the divine,
Saying, "You are free."
The tears you've cried,
Salted and pure,
Are rivers of remembrance,
Of all you endure.
You are the keeper of light,
The spark of the eternal flame,
The salt of the earth,
Uwavering, untamed.
Rise, child of the infinite,
For you are divine by decree.
You are worth your salt,
Whole, holy, and free.

Golden Doorway

Golden Doorway

Standing at the doorway, I pause,
A bridge between now and what will be.
My future self stands radiant, whole,
A vision of dreams calling to me.
The life I see is vast and bright,
So different from my current plight.
Yet I send my request to Heaven's gate,
Resting in trust—it's never too late.
I know I'm heard; I feel it's done,
My path aligned with the rising sun.
With steady breath and heart anew,
I open the door and step on through.
Into my dream, I boldly stride,
A golden world where faith resides.
Transformed, I stand in love's embrace,
A new beginning, a sacred space.

Through the Eyes of the Divine

Through the Eyes of the Divine

If you only knew
That God was looking through your eyes,
Each glance would soften,
Each word would wrap itself in grace,
And every thought would bow
To the sacredness of your being.
If you only knew,
You would hold yourself
As the fragile, luminous vessel you are,
Cradling every flaw with reverence,
Every ache with love,
For even your shadows bear the mark of divinity.
And little did we know,
That the other—
The stranger, the friend, the foe—
Is God, too, peering back,
Through their eyes,
Through their joys and wounds.
We meet divinity in disguise,
A thousand faces reflecting
infinity's eyes.
Would we not tread more gently?
Speak with softer tongues,
And weave compassion into the fabric of every moment?
If you only knew,
You would see the mirror,
in every gaze,
And know—
We are God,
Looking at God,
Forever awakening.

The Day I Saw Heaven in My Own Eyes

The Day I Saw Heaven in My Own Eyes

It wasn't in the sky,
No clouds parted to reveal golden gates.
It was here, on this quiet earth,
In the breath between moments,
Where stillness whispered truth.
I saw it in the shimmer of sunlight
Dancing on leaves,
In the laughter of a child,
Pure, untamed, eternal.
I felt it in the warmth of a hand
Reaching for mine,
In the silent knowing
That I am never alone.
It wasn't distant, nor grand,
But tender, close, and soft.
Heaven wasn't a place that day—
It was a presence,
A remembering.
In my own reflection,
Through tear-streaked eyes,
I saw the spark of something infinite,
A light that had never dimmed,
A love that had never left.
The day I saw Heaven,
I saw myself
As I truly am—
A part of the eternal,
Whole, worthy, divine.

This Is Your Winning Season

This Is Your Winning Season

The tides have turned, the path is clear,
No more waiting, no more fear.
The lessons shaped, the trials faced,
Now step into strength, move with grace.
Every tear became a seed,
Planted deep for what you need.
Can you feel it? Can you see?
The breakthrough forming endlessly.
Doors once locked now swing wide,
Fate and favor walk beside.
What was delayed was never denied,
Your spirit steady, your soul untied.
Are you ready? Can you stand
To claim the life that's in your hands?
You are the storm, you are the flame,
Destiny calls—do you know your name?
This is your winning season—
Wear your crown, trust the reason.
You were made for this, you were born to shine,
The victory was always divine.

Heaven, Take My Breath Away

Heaven, Take My Breath Away

Heaven, take my breath away,
Fill my days with wonder and grace.
Let awe wrap itself around my heart,
And lead me forward with a fresh start.
Show me beauty I can't ignore,
Moments that stir my soul to its core.
Let the mountains speak of something divine,
And the stars remind me I'm always aligned.
Guide my steps with gentle care,
Through the chaos, through the wear.
Let rivers flow as whispers of love,
A quiet song sent from above.
Great Divine, fill my life with peace,
A sense of calm, a sweet release.
Breathe into me a deeper way,
To see the magic in each day.
Take my breath, and fill my soul,
With the light that makes me whole.
May I stand in wonder, fully alive,
Led by grace, where dreams arrive.

Grace, Grit, and Glory

Grace, Grit, and Glory

Through trials that cut like the sharpest knife,
I walk the edge of this fragile life.
With grace to soften each heavy blow,
And grit to rise when the storm winds grow.
I stumble, I fall, yet still I stand,
The strength of the earth in my trembling hands.
The scars I bear are my story's proof,
That through the pain, I've found my truth.
Glory isn't in perfection's glow,
But in the fire that helps us grow.
In the moments we choose to keep pressing on,
Through the darkest nights to meet the dawn.
Grace lifts me, grit holds me steady,
And for glory's call, my heart stays ready.
Through it all, I've come to see—
This is the warrior's legacy in me.

The Fulfillment Within

The Fulfillment Within

The only fulfillment I find is within,
Where silence ends and truths begin.
No fleeting treasure, no worldly praise,
Can match the light my soul displays.
Deep in the stillness, I come to know,
A well of peace that ceaselessly flows.
No outside longing, no searching wide,
For all I need is here inside.
The noise of the world may call my name,
Its promises hollow, its pleasures the same.
Yet in my heart, a quiet voice speaks,
A wisdom eternal, the solace I seek.
It's not in the fleeting or what I gain,
But in the love that soothes my pain.
Each breath, a bridge to the sacred divine,
Each moment, a chance to realign.
A sacred wholeness, steady and true,
The fulfillment within is where I renew.
In the stillness, I stand, grounded and free,
Held by the infinite flowing through me.

Holy Armor

Holy Armor

I laid down my weapons, the burdens I bore,
The shields of defense I carried before.
No sword is needed, no battle to fight,
For joy is my fortress, my guiding light.
All I need is my holy armor,
A heart unbroken, a soul grown calmer.
Faith as my shield, love as my guide,
Truth as the strength I hold inside.
The walls I built, I now release,
To step into grace, to live in peace.
For the war was within, the strife my own,
But now I stand where light is sown.
With holy armor, I face the day,
In love's protection, I find my way.
No fear, no doubt, can steal my song,
For in this truth, I am forever strong.

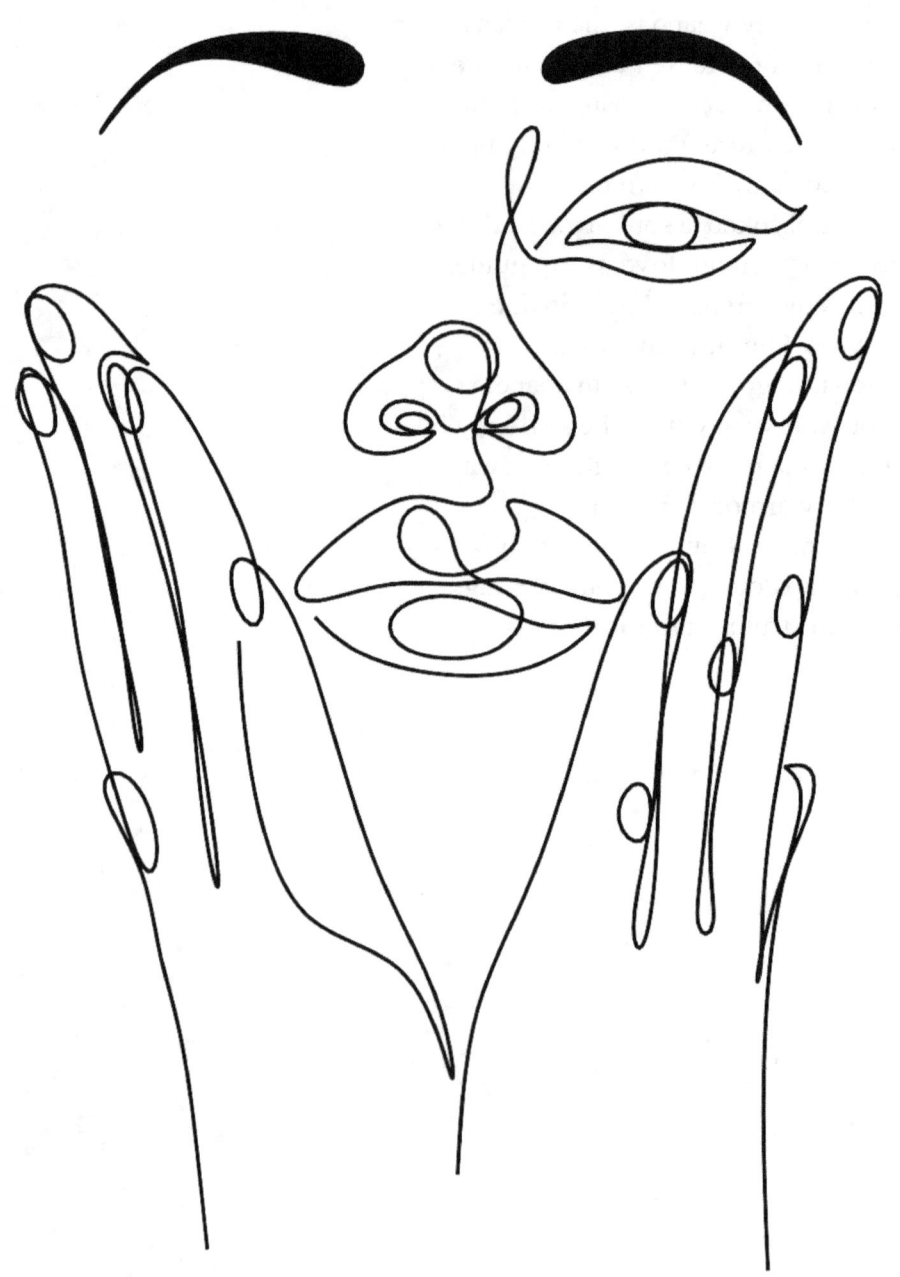

Holy Hands That Heal

Holy Hands That Heal

Holy hands that heal, unseen yet near,
Guiding the weary through pain and fear.
Touching wounds both deep and old,
Transforming the broken into something whole.
In the silence, their power is known,
Mending fractures we thought our own.
They cradle the heart, they soothe the soul,
Restoring the parts we lost to the toll.
Through darkness, they reach with gentle grace,
Carving light into the shadowed space.
A tender touch, a sacred embrace,
Holy hands remind us of love's true face.
Not bound by flesh, nor marked by time,
They bridge the mortal to the divine.
Holy hands that heal, still and strong,
Writing new verses to an ancient song.
With every touch, a story unfolds,
Of redemption, of courage, of truths retold.
Holy hands that heal, unseen yet real,
Teaching us what it means to feel.

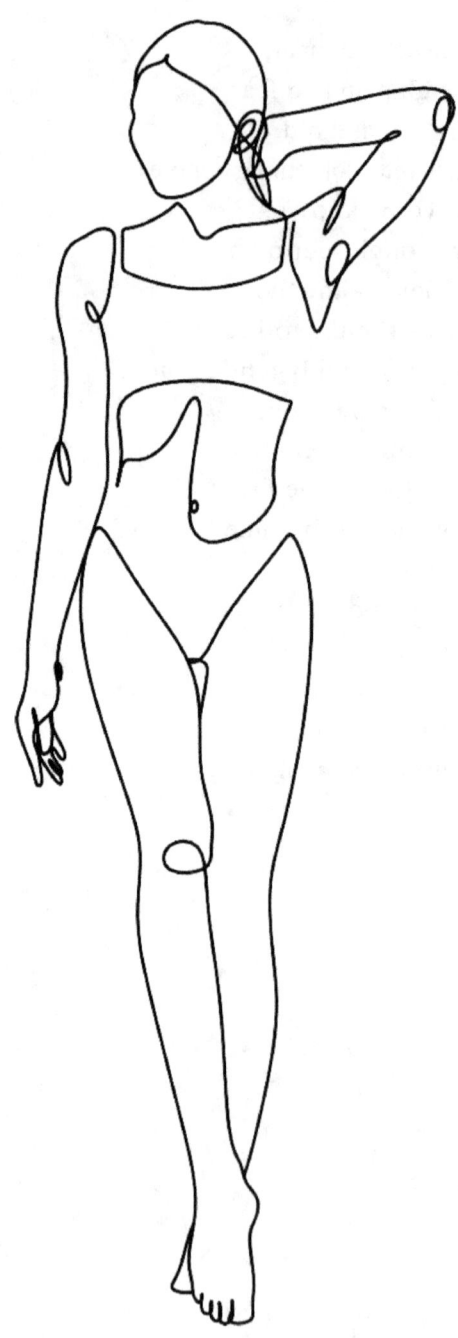

Standing in the Middle of the Zero Point

Standing in the Middle of the Zero Point

Standing in the middle of the zero point,
Where all is still, and yet, all is alive,
The universe breathes in perfect silence,
And we remember who we are, who we've always been.
No past, no future, just this eternal now,
A place where all time converges and dissolves,
Where the soul feels the pulse of creation,
And the heart knows its boundless power.
In the center, we are both everything and nothing,
The weight of the world, the lightness of being.
We stand as witness to the birth of infinity,
As the void cradles us in its infinite embrace.
We are the stars, the dust, the breath of existence,
A symphony of forgotten magnificence,
Awakening to the truth that has always been,
That in this moment, we are home.
Beyond the illusion of separation and space,
We are the cosmic dance of love and grace,
Standing, breathing, knowing—
The zero point is the place we return to,
The place we've never truly left.

Dare to Be Brave

Dare to Be Brave

There is a fire within you,
ancient and untamed,
not meant to flicker, not meant to yield,
but to rise, to roar, to remind the world
that you were never meant to be ordinary.
Not everyone will understand your light.
Some will turn away,
some will question,
some will ask you to quiet the thunder in your soul.
But you were not made for smallness.
You were made to stand, to walk boldly,
to carve a path that has never been walked before.
Dare to be brave.
Dare to hold your ground when the winds howl against you.
Dare to walk alone if it means staying true.
Dare to let your spirit blaze,
not for permission, not for acceptance,
but because it is the only way you were ever meant to exist.
It is no small thing to be fully yourself,
to carry the weight of your own truth
and speak it aloud when the world demands silence.
But the fire within you is sacred,
it was placed there with purpose,
and it will not go out—not for fear, not for doubt,
not for anyone who cannot see its brilliance.
So let them watch.
Let them wonder.
Let them say you are too much.
And let them be right.
Because the bravest thing you will ever do
is refuse to be anything other than exactly who you are.

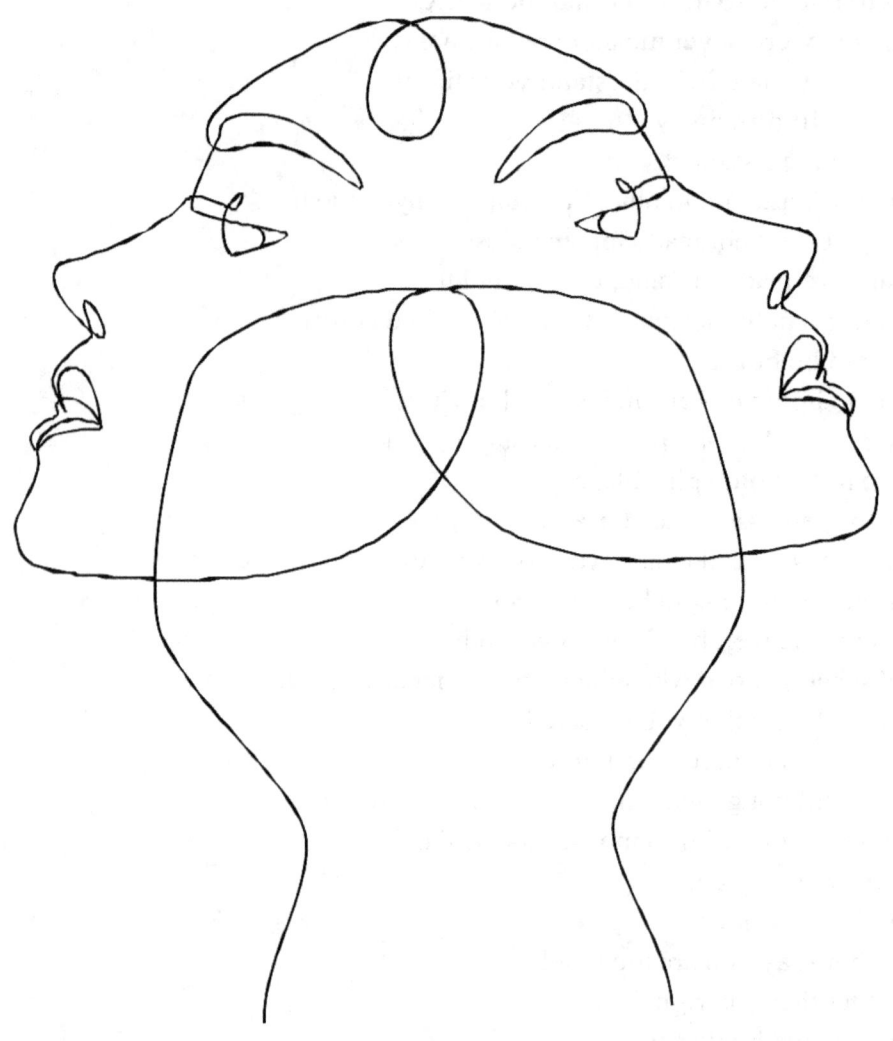

Congruency of the Heart and Mind

Congruency of the Heart and Mind

The heart speaks in soft utterances,
the mind in debate,
One feels the calling, the other hesitates.
Yet in their tension, in their divide,
Lies the key to the sacred, where truth must reside.
The mind maps roads, charts paths so wise,
But the heart knows the way beyond disguise.
When one moves forward, the other must stay,
And so we wander, lost in the fray.
But when heart and mind dance as one,
A bridge is formed, the journey begun.
No longer torn by fear or desire,
They weave creation, they spark the fire.
For thought alone will build but walls,
And feeling alone may lead to falls.
Yet when they meet, both strong and true,
Magic unfolds in all that you do.
So bring them together, let them align,
Let mind trust the heart, and heart trust the mind.
For only in harmony do we create,
A life of purpose, a love that is great.

Sometimes We Don't Get to Know Why

Sometimes We Don't Get to Know Why

We ache for answers, grasping at meaning,
searching for patterns in the midnight sky.
We beg the heavens to reveal reason,
but sometimes, we don't get to know why.
The storm does not explain its thunder,
the ocean never justifies its tide.
The stars do not answer for their falling,
nor does the wind confess where it hides.
We want the closure, the final chapter,
the comfort of knowing how it all aligns.
But life moves in ways beyond our vision,
a masterpiece unfinished by design.
So let the questions rest in silence,
let the mystery teach instead of wound.
Not every thread will show its weaving,
but trust—the pattern is being wound.
Sometimes the answer is in the waiting,
sometimes in learning how to let go.
Not every why was meant to be given,
but every step still helps you grow.

You Are the One Who Has Come to Save Yourself

You Are the One Who Has Come to Save Yourself

Don't be shocked when no one comes to save you,
when the silence meets your cries,
when the world keeps moving forward,
not pausing to lift you from the tides.
Because, my love, you were never meant to wait,
never meant to plead for a guiding hand.
You are the one who has come to save yourself,
the one who will learn to rise and stand.
No one can walk this road for you,
no one can hold your power but you.
This journey was never about being rescued—
it was always about remembering what's true.
The fire you've walked through didn't burn you,
it cleared the path for what you're meant to be.
You were not broken—you were becoming,
learning what it means to be free.
You are the light you have been searching for,
the steady ground beneath your feet.
You are not lost, you are not waiting—
you are arriving, whole and complete.

Only Love Can Walk Through Fire

Only Love Can Walk Through Fire

Only love can walk through fire
without feeling the sting of its burn.
It does not retreat from the heat,
nor cower when the flames return.
It does not flinch at ruin's touch,
nor tremble when the embers glow.
For love was never made of flesh—
it is the breath of all we know.
The fire may rage, consume, and test,
but love remains, it does not fall.
What isn't true will turn to dust,
but love will stand above it all.
No wound can claim it,
no ash remains—
only love can walk through fire
and shine untouched within the flames.

Do Not Underestimate Your Strength

Do Not Underestimate Your Strength

Do not underestimate your strength,
for when you do,
you underestimate the power of God within you.
The force that breathed the stars to life,
that moves the oceans and lifts the sun,
is the same force that pulses in your veins,
that beats within your heart.
You were not made small,
not meant to bend beneath fear.
You are the reflection of the divine,
a flame that will not disappear.
So stand in your knowing,
walk in your light,
for the strength you seek is already inside,
placed there by the hands of creation itself.

When You Have Nothing to Hide, You Become a Very Dangerous Human

When You Have Nothing to Hide, You Become a Very Dangerous Human

They tremble in shadows, fearing the light,
Clutching their masks, holding them tight.
But you stand bare, unchained, unafraid,
A soul with nothing left to evade.
No secrets bind, no shame restrains,
No weight of guilt, no rusted chains.
You walk unburdened, stripped to the bone,
Owning every scar as if it were stone.
You become a very dangerous human—
Not for the harm you could ever inflict,
But for the truth you refuse to restrict.
A heart unshackled, a mind set free,
Terrifies those still bound by deceit.
They fear the ones who cannot be swayed,
Who stand unshaken, who won't be played.
For a human with nothing left to disguise
Is one who sees through all the lies.
You speak, and the walls begin to crack,
Not with force, but the weight of fact.
You look them straight into their eyes,
And watch as their illusions die.
For nothing is more fearsome, nothing more free,
Than the one who dares to simply be.
Unburdened, unyielding, standing alone—
A force of truth, fully known.

Poetic Alchemy

Poetic Alchemy

I take the weight of all I've carried,
the sorrow, the longing, the scars unseen.
I lay them down upon the altar,
letting fire make them clean.
What was once pain becomes wisdom,
what was once fear turns into light.
The ink of my story, once written in shadow,
now burns with gold in the dead of night.
I stir the silence, shape the echoes,
forge new meaning from the past.
For even the wounds that tried to break me
have become poetry that will forever last.
This is the alchemy of becoming,
where the broken turns to whole.
Where suffering bows before the artist,
and words become the healer's soul.

Beyond the Surface

Beyond the Surface

Beyond the surface, I see myself whole,
Deep with love that forever holds my soul.
I see my depths, a truth only I know,
Reaching my essence, where eternal light glows.
Beyond the surface, my stillness runs deep,
Whispers of wisdom in silence I keep.
My quiet, soft eyes reflect what I see,
A boundless connection to all that is free.
For who I am belongs in the deep,
In the sacred stillness, where mysteries sleep.
A timeless truth, an eternal flame,
Beyond the surface, I am not the same.

Beyond the Dark Night

Beyond the Dark Night

Beyond the night, the dawn awaits,
A softened glow through heaven's gates.
The pain you've carried, the tears you've sown,
Shape the strength you'll call your own.
For darkness only bends the knee
To those who rise, who dare to see,
That even in the void's control,
Lies the passage to a whole, healed soul.
Beyond the dark, your light will shine,
A testament to the divine.
And as you step from shadow's hold,
You'll find yourself reborn, made whole.

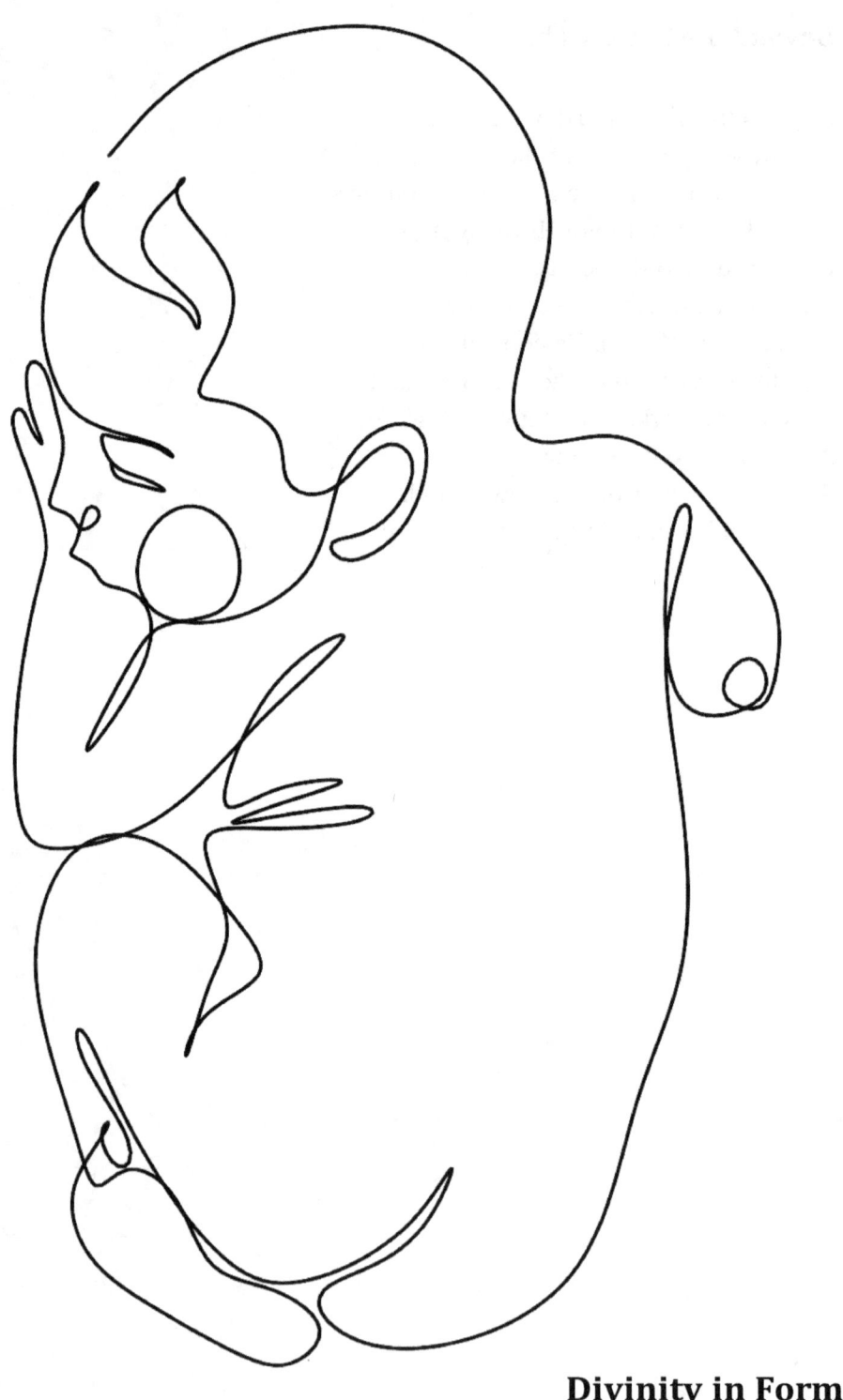

Divinity in Form

Divinity in Form

A child enters the world, untouched by doubt,
Wrapped in the glow of a truth never questioned.
We gaze upon them, their breath a quiet hymn,
And say, pure, whole, a miracle, divine.
Not once do we ask if they are worthy.
Not once do we wonder if their light is real.
We simply know.
Yet time presses in like an unrelenting tide,
Layering over that sacred knowing,
With every wound, every silent doubt,
Every battle fought in the depths of the soul.
The world tells us to forget,
To stay small, to fracture, to question—
To believe divinity is something distant,
Something earned, something lost.
But divinity was never lost.
It only waits beneath the dust of forgetting,
Beneath the weight of all you were told to be,
Of all you thought you had to become.
Let the old names fall from your skin.
Let the wounds become doors, not chains.
Let the false selves burn like morning mist.
You were never less than light.
You were never separate from grace.
You are the same breath, the same wonder,
That entered this world.
You are not waiting to become.
You are not searching to find.
You are what you seek.

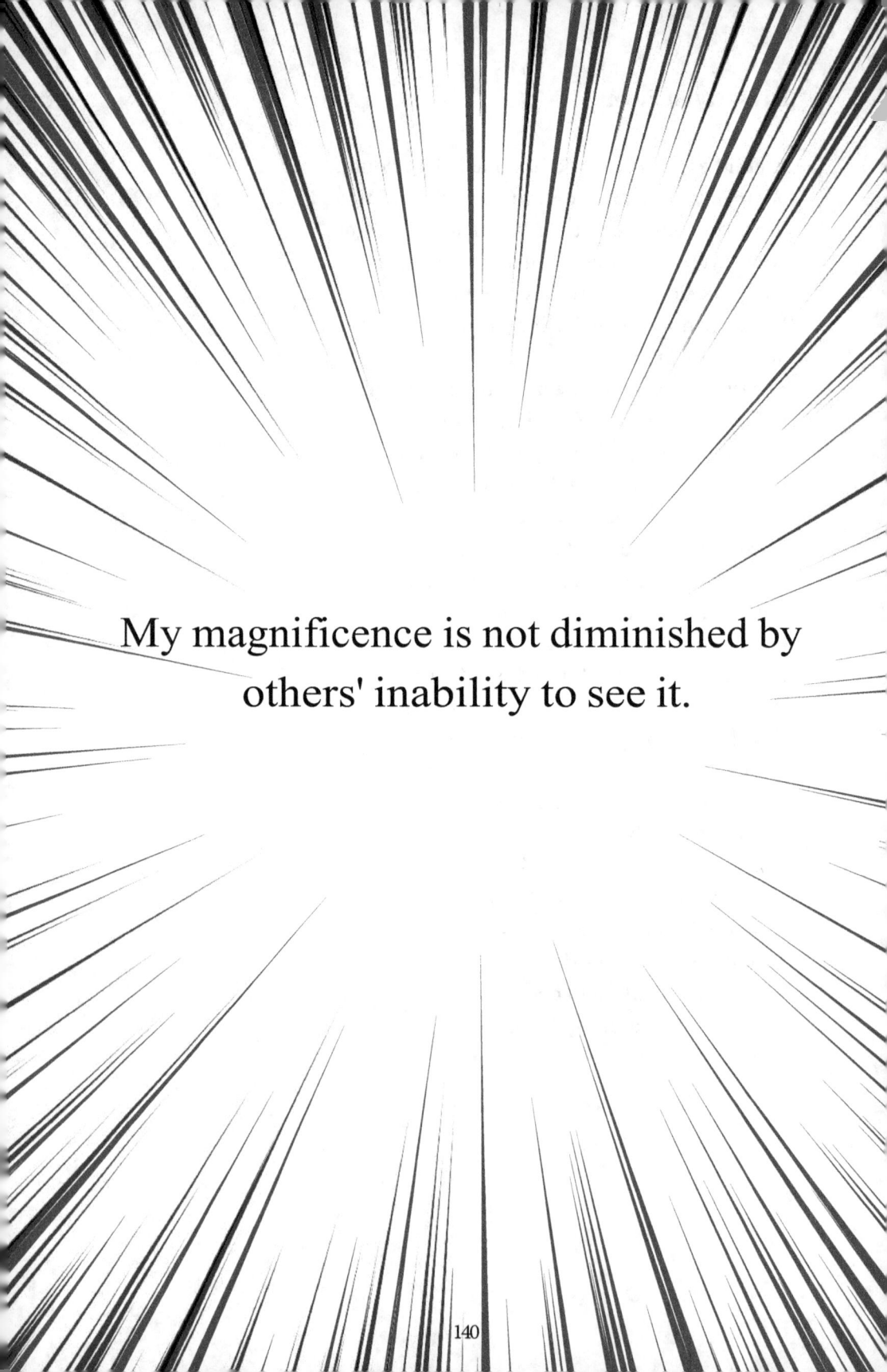

Forgotten Magnificence
Short Stories

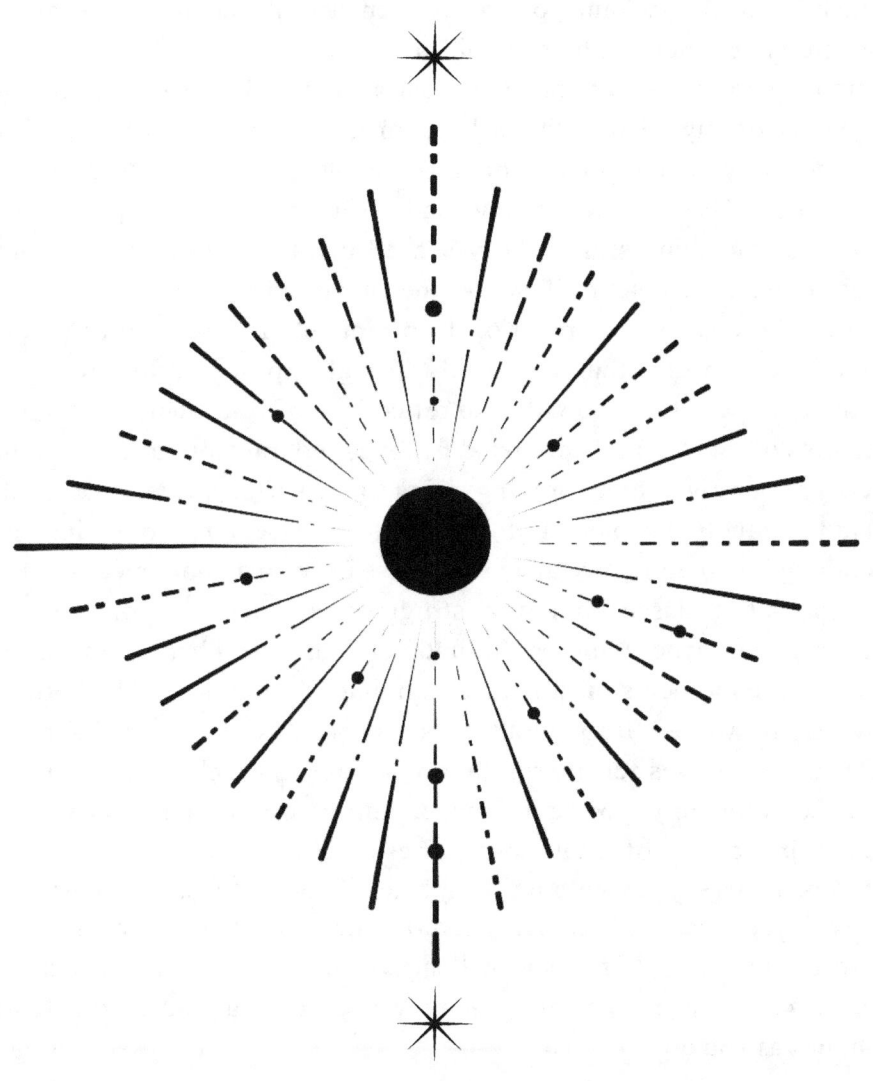

Introduction to the Short Stories of Forgotten Magnificence

Every story holds a secret. Beneath the surface of words, between the lines, and in the pauses where the unsaid lingers—there is always something more.

This second part of Forgotten Magnificence is not simply a collection of short stories; it is an invitation. A doorway into deeper contemplation. A journey into the spaces of life that often go unnoticed. These stories are meant to be felt as much as they are read. They are designed to stir something ancient within you, to awaken truths that may have always been present but never fully recognized.

Some of these stories are not fiction at all but real, lived experiences—fragments of my own path back to magnificence. Names have been changed to honor the privacy of those involved, yet the lessons remain untarnished. These moments, raw and unfiltered, carry weight because they hold something sacred. They shaped me, tested me, and ultimately revealed to me the quiet resilience of the human spirit.

Sharing these stories is an act of deep remembrance, a way of holding space for the wisdom that life reveals through experience. In offering my truth, my hope is that you will find reflections of your own. Through my moments of revelation, heartbreak, healing, and transformation, you may uncover your own quiet knowing rising to the surface. Every soul walks a path uniquely its own, but the essence of seeking, breaking, and becoming is something we all share. These pages may hold pieces of you. Perhaps you will see your own struggles reflected here or sense the unspoken experiences of those around you—the silent battles, the unseen wounds, the moments of quiet triumph that often go unnoticed. Hidden lessons are woven throughout these stories, waiting for discovery, offering themselves for interpretation in ways that only you can define. Because, ultimately, your experience, your emotions, and your wisdom are the final author of what these stories mean.

Approach these pages with an open heart. Read not just with curiosity, but with presence, with empathy. Allow these words to sit with you, to move through you. Let them challenge you, comfort you, expand you. Recognize that every person you meet carries an untold story of their own, just as you do.

There are lessons here, but they are not forced. Truth is scattered throughout these pages, but it does not demand to be seen. Meaning will emerge only when you allow it to, when you give yourself permission to look beyond the surface.

Step in. Feel deeply. Let these stories meet you where you are, and perhaps, take you somewhere new.

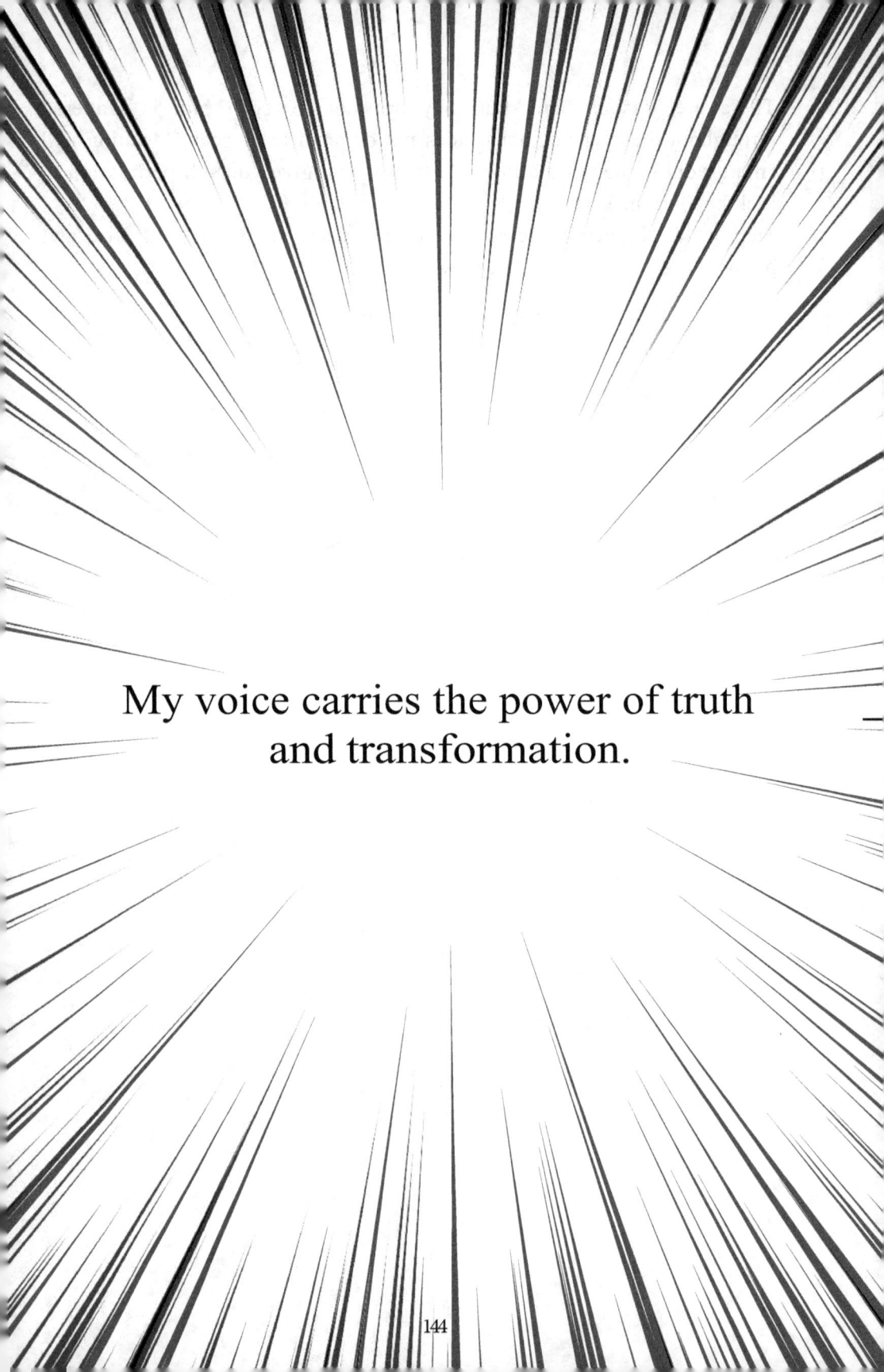

My voice carries the power of truth and transformation.

Unshaken: The Power of Standing in Your Truth

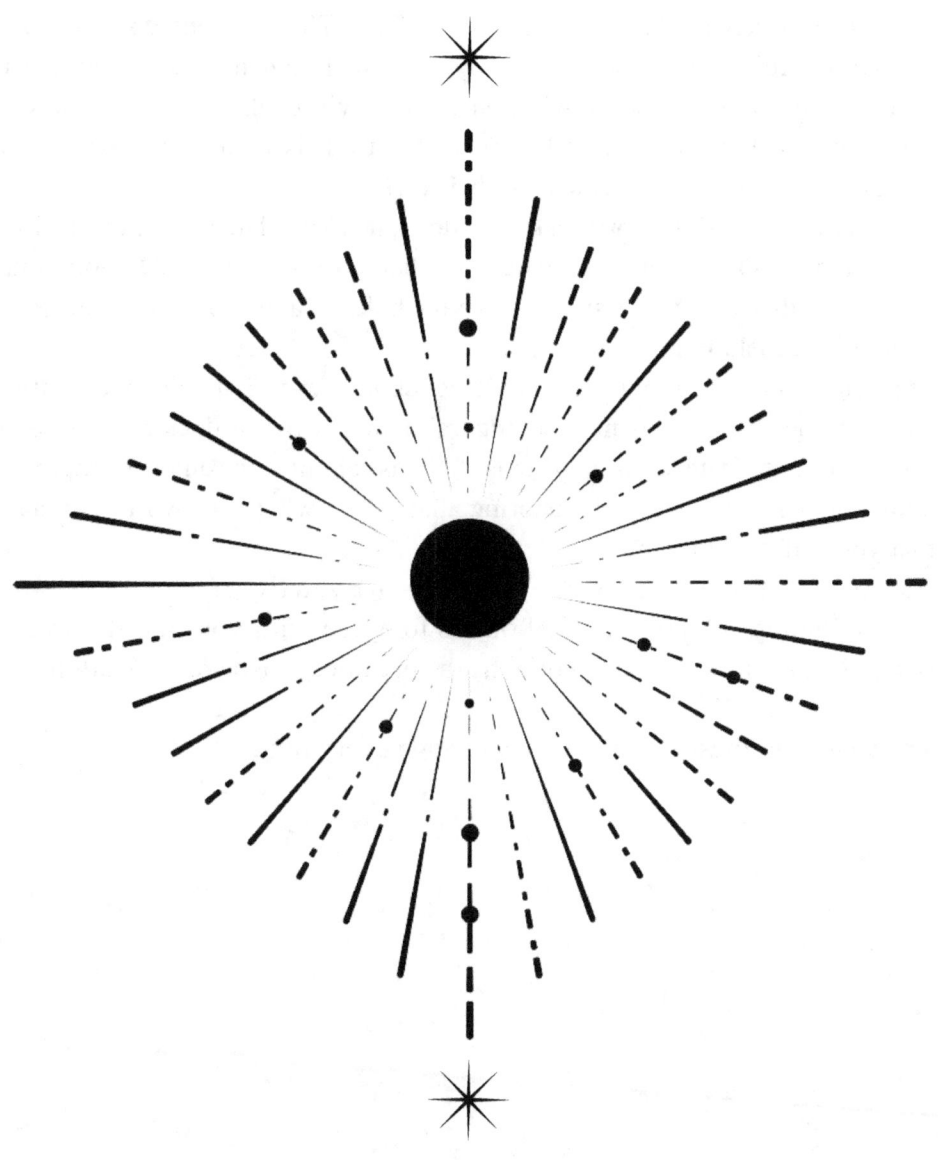

Introduction: Unshaken: The Power of Standing in Your Truth

What happens when you speak your truth, and it offends someone? Have you ever noticed how certain beliefs seem to shake people to their core—not because they are false, but because they challenge something unexamined within them? Why does someone else's certainty make others so uncomfortable? Is it because deep down, they fear that their truth may not be as solid as they once believed?

This is the quiet battle that many of us face. The moment you step into your truth, fully and unapologetically, you will find that not everyone is willing to celebrate it. Some will resist, some will challenge, and some will even try to tear it down. Not because your truth is invalid, but because it forces them to look at the cracks in their own.

So, here's a question worth asking—do you trust what you know inside? Truly trust it? Or do you only believe it when others approve? Do you stand in your truth when it's easy, or can you hold steady when the winds of doubt come rushing in?

This story is not about debate. It is about what happens when truth stands alone—when it is not seeking validation, when it does not beg to be accepted, but instead simply exists. It is about the quiet strength of knowing who you are and honoring that, even when the world demands that you shift to fit its mold.

As you read, I invite you to ask yourself—are you living your truth, or are you defending it? Do you need others to agree with you in order to feel secure? Or can you let your truth breathe, unshaken, needing no permission?

The answer to these questions may change everything.

Unshaken: The Power of Standing in Your Truth

Jack walked the familiar path toward the old library at the heart of town, his thoughts heavy. The last few weeks had been a test of his resilience. Conversations that once felt easy now carried tension. Friends he had known for years now questioned him, ridiculed him even, simply because he had dared to speak his truth. It was a strange thing—how quickly people turned defensive when confronted with something that didn't align with their own beliefs.

As he reached the grand wooden doors, he spotted Owen sitting on the library steps, waiting for him. Jack had known this conversation was inevitable.

"You've changed," Owen said before Jack even had a chance to sit down. His voice was neutral, but his eyes carried something else—concern, maybe even fear.

Jack sighed, lowering himself onto the step beside him. "I haven't changed. I've just stopped pretending."

Owen frowned. "Stopped pretending? What does that mean?"

Jack turned to face him. "It means I no longer shape my truth to fit someone else's expectations. I no longer need the approval of others to validate what I know inside."

Owen ran a hand through his hair, exhaling sharply. "But what if you're wrong? What if everything you believe is just a construct of your own perception?"

Jack gave a small, knowing smile. "Then that's for me to discover. That's the thing about truth, Owen. If it's real, it stands. It doesn't need to be defended, nor does it fear being questioned. It simply is. But let me ask you something—if you were completely secure in what you believe, why does my truth unsettle you so much"

Owen shifted uncomfortably. "It's not that it unsettles me… It's just that it contradicts everything I've been taught. Everything I've built my life around. If I entertain the idea that you might be right, then I have to question everything."

Jack nodded. "And that's terrifying, isn't it? Because then you realize that the truth you were given might not be the truth that was meant for you."

Owen looked away, his jaw tightening. "People don't like uncertainty, Jack. They want firm ground to stand on."

Jack chuckled softly.

"The problem is, most people are standing on borrowed ground, not their own. They cling to what they've been told, never questioning, never seeking. But truth isn't about comfort. It's about alignment. When you know something deep in your soul, you don't need anyone else to agree with it."

Owen shook his head, frustrated. "But what if your truth leads people astray What if it causes division"

Jack's expression softened. "Then those people were never standing firm in their own truth to begin with. A person who truly believes does not need to fight for their truth or force others to conform. They simply live it. The ones who try to control others—those are the ones who fear they might be wrong. Because real truth? It doesn't need a crowd to sustain it."

Silence settled between them. Owen's mind wrestled with Jack's words, but his heart felt something else—a tug, a quiet acknowledgment that Jack might be right.

"So what do you do?" Owen finally asked. "When people come at you, telling you you're wrong, trying to force you to believe what they do?"

Jack took a deep breath. "You listen. Not to argue, not to prove them wrong, but to understand. Then you walk away still knowing what you know. You don't have to shrink yourself to fit someone else's comfort. You don't have to prove anything. Just because someone shouts louder doesn't make them right. If someone is secure in what they believe, they won't be threatened by someone else's perspective."

Owen looked at Jack with something new in his gaze—not frustration, not resistance, but curiosity. "So you're saying that if I fully believe in my truth, yours wouldn't bother me?"

Jack nodded. "Exactly. Because when you fully embrace what you know inside, you stop needing to change anyone else. You stop needing validation. You just live. And you let others do the same."

Owen let out a breath he hadn't realized he was holding. "Maybe I've been defending my beliefs instead of living them."

Jack smiled. "Maybe we all have. But the real power isn't in proving a point—it's in standing firm in who you are, no matter who agrees with you."

Owen considered this, looking up at the sky as if searching for an answer. "So what now?"

Jack stood, dusting off his jeans. "Now, you choose. Will you fight to prove your truth, or will you live it so fully that it needs no defense?"

Owen met his gaze and, for the first time in a long time, felt something settle inside him. "I think I'm ready to just live it."

Jack grinned. "Then you've already won."

The air between them was lighter now, not because all questions had been answered, but because the need to answer them had lessened. The weight of proving, defending, convincing—it had lifted. In its place was something steadier, something truer.

The streetlights flickered on, casting a soft glow over the small town. A breeze moved through the trees, carrying the scent of earth and the hum of a world that had never needed permission to exist exactly as it was. Jack and Owen walked in unspoken understanding, no longer seeking to change or be changed.

Some truths were meant to be lived, not explained. Some battles were never meant to be fought, only surrendered to with quiet certainty.

Jack glanced at Owen, a knowing glint in his eye. "Funny thing about truth—it never actually needs defending. It only ever asks to be honored."

Owen let out a breath, feeling lighter than he had in years. "Maybe that's all any of us are really here to do."

Jack smiled, and together, they stepped forward—not as men who had won or lost an argument, but as men who had freed themselves from the need for one.

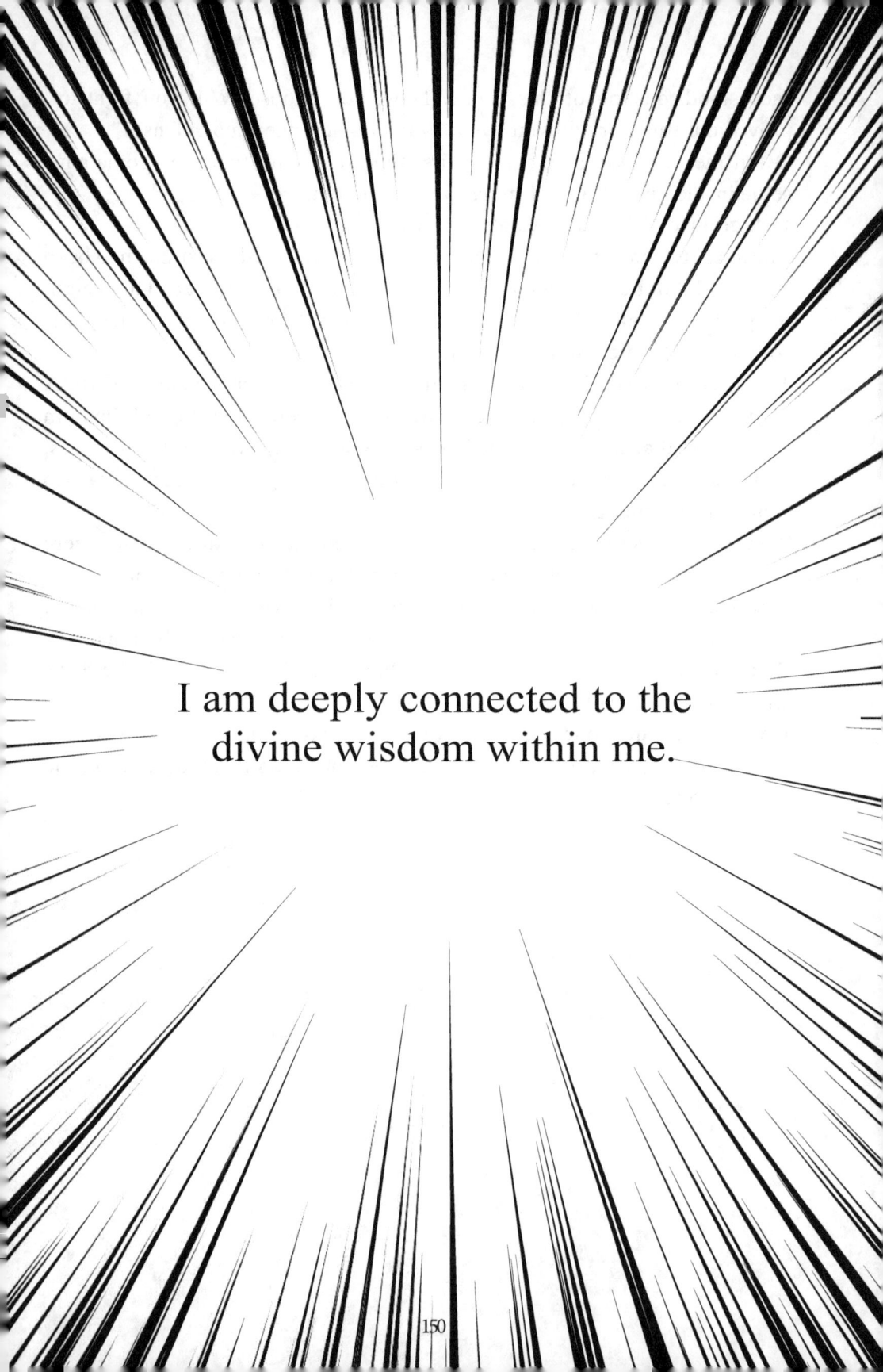

I am deeply connected to the divine wisdom within me.

They Will Never Forget How You Made Them Feel

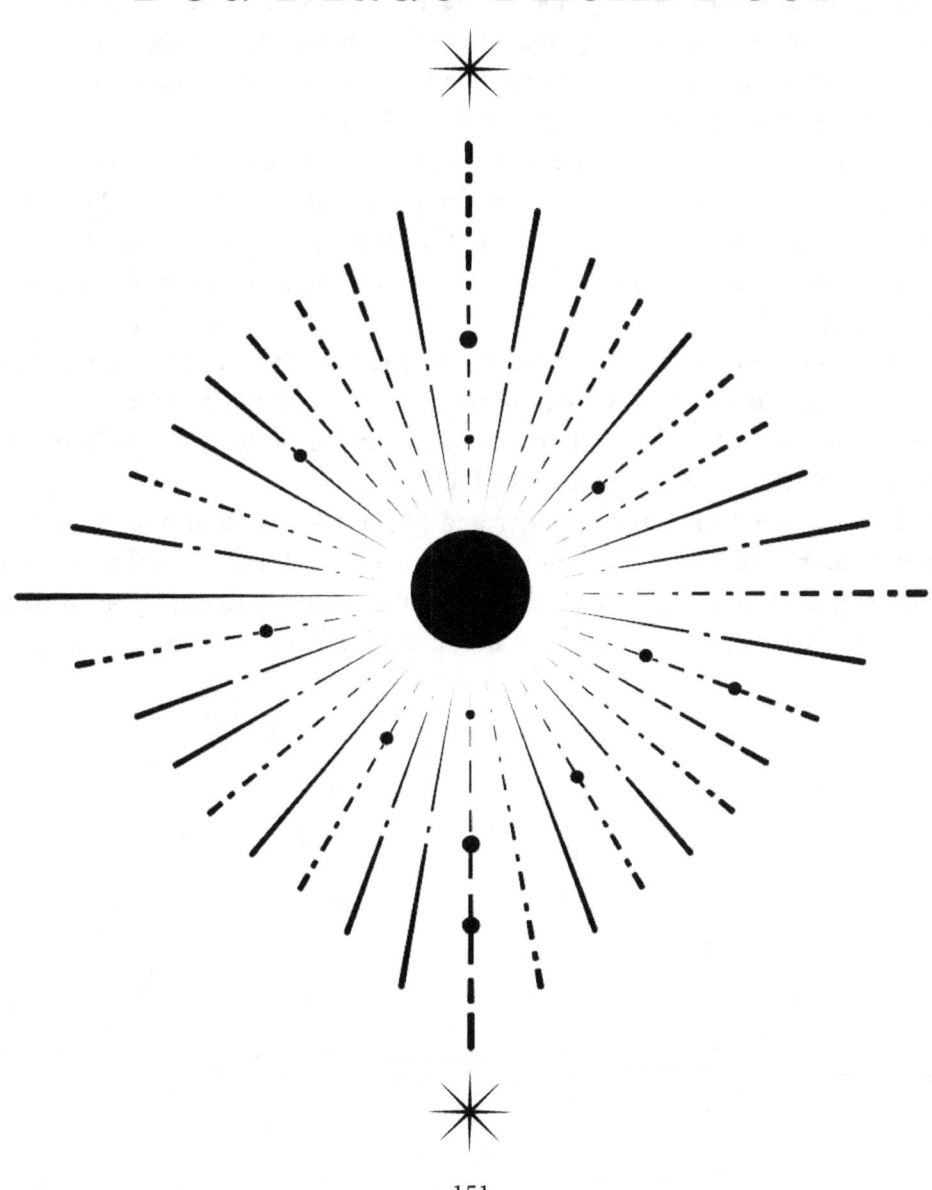

Introduction: They Will Never Forget How You Made Them Feel

There is a quiet power in the way we touch the lives of others. Not through grand gestures, not through words carved in stone, but in the way we make people feel—how we hold space for them, how we see them, how we remind them they matter.

We often believe that our legacy is built upon our accomplishments, the milestones we reach, or the recognition we receive. But in truth, the most lasting imprint we leave behind is the feeling we give others when they stand in our presence. They may forget what we did. They may forget what we said. But they will never forget how we made them feel.

This story is a reflection of that truth. It is a reminder that the smallest kindness, the simplest moment of presence, can change the course of someone's life in ways we may never fully understand. It speaks to the sacred responsibility we hold in every interaction—to choose love, to embody grace, and to offer the warmth of our presence in a world that can often feel cold.

It also invites you to reflect on your own journey. Who has made you feel safe, seen, and worthy? Whose presence lingers in your heart long after they have left the room? Perhaps most importantly, how will others remember the way you made them feel?

This story is not just about Archer and Miriam—it is about all of us. It is about the power of simple moments, the weight of a quiet smile, and the sacred gift of being truly present for another. May it remind you of your own ability to leave an indelible mark on the hearts of those you meet.

They Will Never Forget How You Made Them Feel

There was a small town nestled between two great mountains, where the sun set in hues of gold, and the river sang a song only the wise could hear. It was a place where time moved gently, where people greeted each other with sincerity, and where the past and present intertwined like vines on an ancient willow tree.

In this village, there lived an old woman named Miriam. She was neither the wealthiest nor the strongest, nor did she hold any title of great importance. Yet, she was known by all. Not for what she had accomplished, but for how she made people feel.

She would sit each morning on the steps of her front porch, sipping a cup of tea, offering quiet smiles and warm nods to passersby. She listened when others spoke, not just with her ears but with her entire being. When she looked at you, it felt as though she saw something beyond the flesh—something deeper, something sacred.

One day, a teenage boy named Archer walked into the village square, shoulders hunched, hands stuffed deep into his pockets. He had been carrying the weight of ridicule, the sharp sting of words spoken to wound. He was tired—tired of trying to fight back, tired of pretending that the world didn't hurt him. The boys at school saw him as weak, a target for their unkindness. No matter how hard he tried to be indifferent, it cut him deeper than he wanted to admit.

As he walked past Miriam's front porch, close to the village square, something made him stop. She was looking at the sky, her eyes soft but unwavering. It was as if she saw something beyond what was in front of her.

"What are you looking at?" he asked.

Miriam turned to him, her expression warm and knowing. "The sky moves as it always has, yet no cloud is ever the same. The wind carries them forward, reshaping them as they go. Much like us."

Archer exhaled sharply. "People don't change. They stay the same, stuck in who they are. Some people are just cruel."

Miriam regarded him thoughtfully, then said, "The sun shines on the sinner and the saint alike. Life gives us all the same light, but it is we who decide how to carry it."

Archer's expression tightened. "What's that supposed to mean? That I should just let people walk all over me?

That I should just keep taking it?"

Miriam shook her head. "No, my dear. But do not let them make you forget who you are. You have a choice in what you carry forward. The way you make others feel will always be remembered more than the words they throw at you. That does not excuse their behavior, but it frees you from being chained to it. Hold love in your heart for them, not because they deserve it, but because you deserve the peace that love brings."

Archer let the words sink in. He had spent so much time trying to be tough, trying to prove he was not weak. But what if strength was not in how much he could take, but in how much he could still give?

As the days passed, Archer found himself drawn to Miriam's presence. He saw how people left her side lighter, how she had a way of making them feel seen. A widow who had lost her husband found solace in her stillness. A merchant who had suffered losses sat with her in silence and left with renewed strength. A child who had been scolded found reassurance in a simple touch on the shoulder.

One evening, as the sky burned with the colors of a setting sun, Archer turned to Miriam. "How do you do it? You change people, and yet you do nothing."

Miriam chuckled softly. "I do not seek to change anyone. I simply meet them as they are. No judgment, no expectation—only presence. Love, my dear, is not in grand gestures. It is in the way we hold space for others, allowing them to feel seen, safe, and valued. That is what remains. That is what they will carry long after I am gone."

Archer let those words settle deep within him. For the first time, he understood. Not everything needed to be proven, not everything needed to be remembered in words. The only true legacy was how deeply one had loved, how freely one had given light to another.

Years later, long after Miriam had passed, the village still spoke of her kindness. When young boys came to the village square carrying the weight of the world on their shoulders, they often found a man sitting on the same front porch, offering a quiet smile, a warm nod. His name was Archer, and though few remembered where he had come from, many would always remember how he made them feel. He did not try to be something grand. He did not try to change the world. He simply existed in such a way that made the world around him lighter.

In the end, that was enough.

Archer came to understand that presence itself was an offering, a quiet revolution in a world that so often overlooked the power of kindness. He lived not to be remembered for his achievements, nor to carve his name into the town's history, but to leave a lingering warmth in the hearts of those who crossed his path.

Over the years, his presence became a steady force—like the wind that moved through the valley, unseen yet felt by all. The children who once passed by in hurried steps grew older and carried with them the feeling of being seen, of being acknowledged. The merchant who once sat with Miriam found himself offering comfort to another, passing on the simple yet profound gift of being fully present.

Archer realized that Miriam had not taught him how to change the world; she had taught him how to be in it. Not through words, nor through grand actions, but through the quiet, unwavering love that outlives the fleeting moments of our lives. He understood now that people may not remember the exact words he spoke or the gestures he made, but they would always remember how he made them feel—lighter, seen, and worthy.

As the years passed and the seasons changed, Archer continued to sit on that porch, his presence a silent invitation to anyone who needed it. And so, Miriam's lesson lived on, not as a story embedded into history, but as something far greater—an imprint on the soul, carried forward in the hearts of those who had been touched by it.

For love, in its quietest form, was the only thing that ever truly endured.

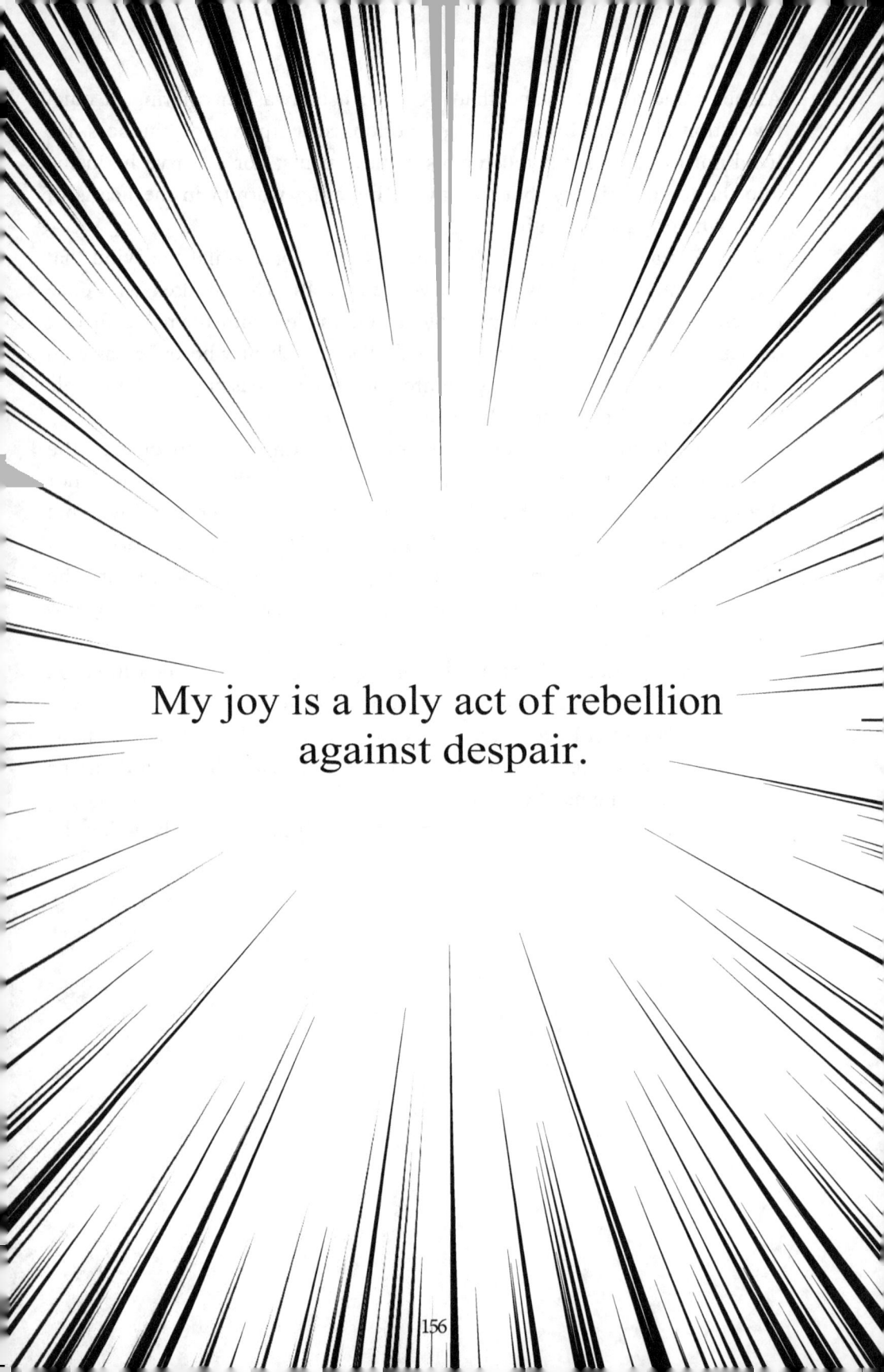

You Can't Fix What Was Never Broken

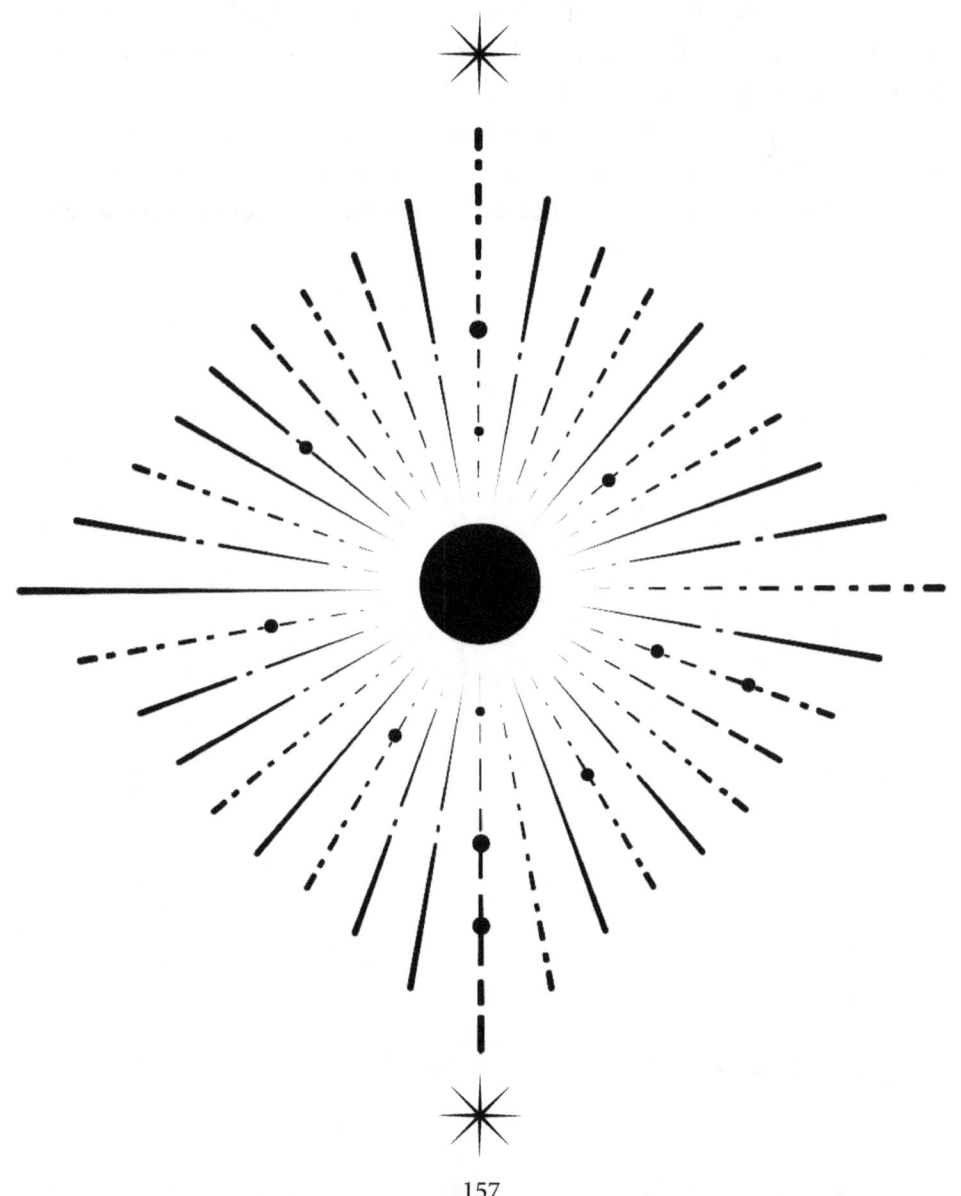

Introduction: You Can't Fix What Was Never Broken

At some point in our journey when we all pause and ask ourselves—Am I broken? We carry wounds, regrets, and lingering remnants of past pain, believing that somehow, we are fractured, incomplete, in need of fixing. But what if the very premise of that belief is false? What if, beneath the weight of our struggles, we were never broken at all?

This story is a reminder that the soul is untouched by time, unmarked by hardship, and immune to the illusions of inadequacy. We are not something that needs repairing—we are something that needs remembering. The journey is not about piecing ourselves back together but uncovering the wholeness that has always been within us.

Healing is not about fixing what is damaged—it is about recognizing what was never lost. And sometimes, the most profound truth comes not in the search for answers but in the quiet realization that we were always whole.

You Can't Fix What Was Never Broken

Ezra sat on the wooden bench in the middle of the park, his hands folded neatly on his lap, his eyes lost somewhere beyond the horizon. He had the kind of presence that made people pause without knowing why—as if wisdom itself sat beside him.

Violet, her shoulders heavy with an invisible weight, approached hesitantly. Something about him felt safe, familiar, though they had never met. She sat beside him, letting silence settle before she spoke.

"I don't know why, but I feel like I can talk to you," she admitted, staring at her hands. "I feel broken."

Ezra nodded as if he had heard this many times before. "Why do you believe that?"

She exhaled, her voice trembling. "Because I carry things I can't let go of. Because my past haunts me. Because no matter how much I try to fix myself, something still feels missing."

Ezra was quiet for a long moment before he finally said, "Tell me, child, if you take a seed and plant it in the soil, does it think itself broken because it has not yet bloomed?"

The young woman's brow furrowed slightly as she considered his words. "No... It's just growing."

He smiled. "Exactly. And yet, here you sit, judging yourself for not being something you were never meant to be—not yet, anyway."

She blinked back tears. "But I feel like something inside me is shattered."

Ezra studied her carefully, then reached into his pocket, pulling out a smooth stone. "Do you see this?"

She nodded.

"I found this on the shore many years ago. The ocean has been shaping it for centuries, smoothing its edges, refining its form. If you had seen it long ago, it would have been jagged and rough. But was it ever broken?"

She shook her head slowly.

He placed the stone in her palm, his voice gentle. "You are not broken, either. You are being shaped. Life is the tide that smooths you, not to fix you, but to reveal what was always there."

Tears welled in her eyes. "But the pain, the scars... they make me feel less than whole."

He tilted his head, his expression full of understanding. "What if you are only identifying with the part of you that was never meant to define you? The soul is untouched by time, circumstance, or wounds. It cannot be fractured. The only part of you that can feel broken is the part that believes in limitation—the part that clings to the idea that something is missing."

She looked down at the stone in her hand, tracing its surface with her fingers. "So, you're saying I don't need fixing?"

Ezra chuckled. "No, my dear. You need remembering. You are not something broken in need of repair. You are something whole, unfolding, becoming."

She let his words settle deep into her being. The weight she had carried for so long—the belief that she was less than, incomplete—began to loosen its grip.

Ezra continued, "The world teaches you to seek healing as if you were shattered, but true healing is simply remembering your wholeness. The soul was never harmed. Only the mind believes it has been wounded."

A quiet strength grew inside her, replacing the doubt that once lived there. She wiped her tears and looked at Ezra with gratitude. "Thank you."

He simply nodded, his gaze drifting back to the horizon. "Go live, child. The world does not need another person trying to be perfect. It needs more people who understand they were never broken to begin with."

She walked away with lighter steps, the stone still warm in her hand, a reminder that she was whole, just as she was.

Let Me Show You Love Exists

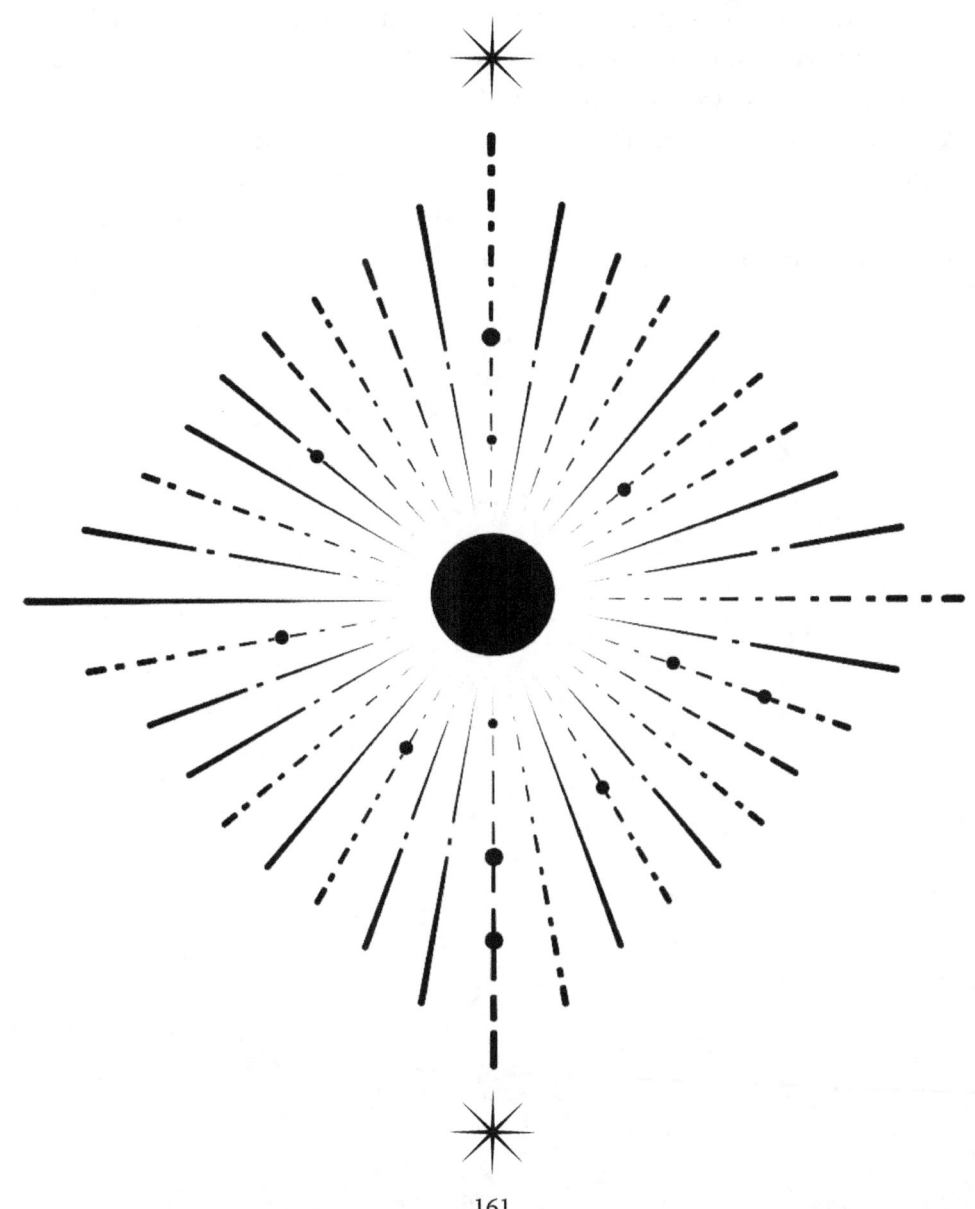

Introduction: Let Me Show You Love Exists

There are moments in life when we hold too tightly to logic, demanding proof before we allow ourselves to believe. We crave certainty, tangible evidence, and something we can point to and say, there it is. But love, in its truest form, does not always arrive with proof. It does not need validation—it simply is.

This story offers a slightly cheeky way to explore this truth, gently challenging the part of us that hesitates, that doubts what the heart already knows. It reminds us that not everything in life can be weighed or measured, yet some things, like love, faith, and the unseen forces that move through us, are the most real of all.

As you read, let yourself soften into the knowing that love is not something to be captured—it is something to be experienced. It does not need to be seen to be known. And perhaps, by the end of this story, you won't just understand that—you'll feel it.

Let Me Show You Love Exists

Do you believe love exists?
Not as a fleeting thought, not as a word spoken in passing, but as something undeniable? Something as real as the ground beneath your feet, as the breath in your lungs?
If I were to hold out my hand and ask you to place love in my palm—right here, where I could see it, weigh it, hold it—what would you do? How would you prove that love is real?
You might offer examples—a mother holding her newborn, the way two hands instinctively find each other in the dark, the silent understanding between old friends. But if I asked again, Where is it? Place it in my hand, you would realize—love cannot be held, yet it holds everything together.
This is the paradox of love. This is the nature of faith. We demand proof of the unseen while living every day under its influence.
Let me tell you a story.
There was once a blind man named Daniel. He had never seen the stars, never known the way sunlight spills across the ocean, never witnessed the changing colors of autumn. Yet, he had never questioned that these things existed. Others spoke of them, and he believed. He had faith in their words.
One evening, a traveler came to his village, a man who prided himself on reason. He had studied science, measured the world, and believed only in what could be proven. The two sat together beneath the night sky.
The traveler said, "You have never seen the stars. How do you know they are real?"
Daniel smiled. "Because I have felt their presence in the cool hush of night, in the way the world changes under their watch. I hear them in the stillness. I know they are there."
The traveler shook his head. "That is not enough. If you cannot see something, how can you know it exists?"
Daniel turned toward him. "Then tell me—do you believe love exists?"
"Of course," the traveler scoffed.
Daniel held out his hands. "Then place it here."
The traveler hesitated. "Love is not something you can hold."
"Yet you believe in it?" Daniel asked.
The traveler nodded, unsure of where this was going.

"Then how do you know it is real?" Daniel pressed. "Have you ever weighed it? Measured it? Held it in your hands?"

The traveler's lips parted, but no answer came.

Daniel continued, "I have never seen the stars, but I feel their presence in the whisper of the wind, in the rhythm of the world. I have never seen the ocean, but I hear its song in the waves that reach the shore. You have never held love, yet you have felt its presence. There are things in this world more real than what our hands can grasp. Some truths must be known without proof."

The traveler frowned, his mind grasping at logic, but his heart beginning to understand something deeper.

"Then love, like the stars, like the ocean, like the unseen forces that shape our lives," Daniel continued, "does not need to be proven. It only needs to be known."

The traveler sat quietly, watching the sky above, feeling the weight of what had been said.

For the first time, he realized that much of what he held to be true had no proof at all. He had never seen the wind, yet he felt it against his skin. He had never seen time, yet he knew it passed. He had never seen his own thoughts, yet they shaped his world. And just like these unseen forces, love moved through everything—unnoticed by the eyes, but undeniable to the heart.

The logic he had clung to all his life suddenly felt small, incomplete. He had believed only in what could be measured, but now he saw—some things are beyond measure. Some things are known not by sight, but by experience.

Daniel spoke again, softly. "Love does not need to be proven to exist. It simply is. And once you understand that, you will stop asking for evidence and start living in its presence."

The traveler closed his eyes and let out a breath he didn't realize he had been holding. He felt the night around him, the hum of life, the weight of something vast and unseen pressing gently against him. For the first time in his life, he stopped searching for proof—and simply believed.

While the Embers Are Still Burning

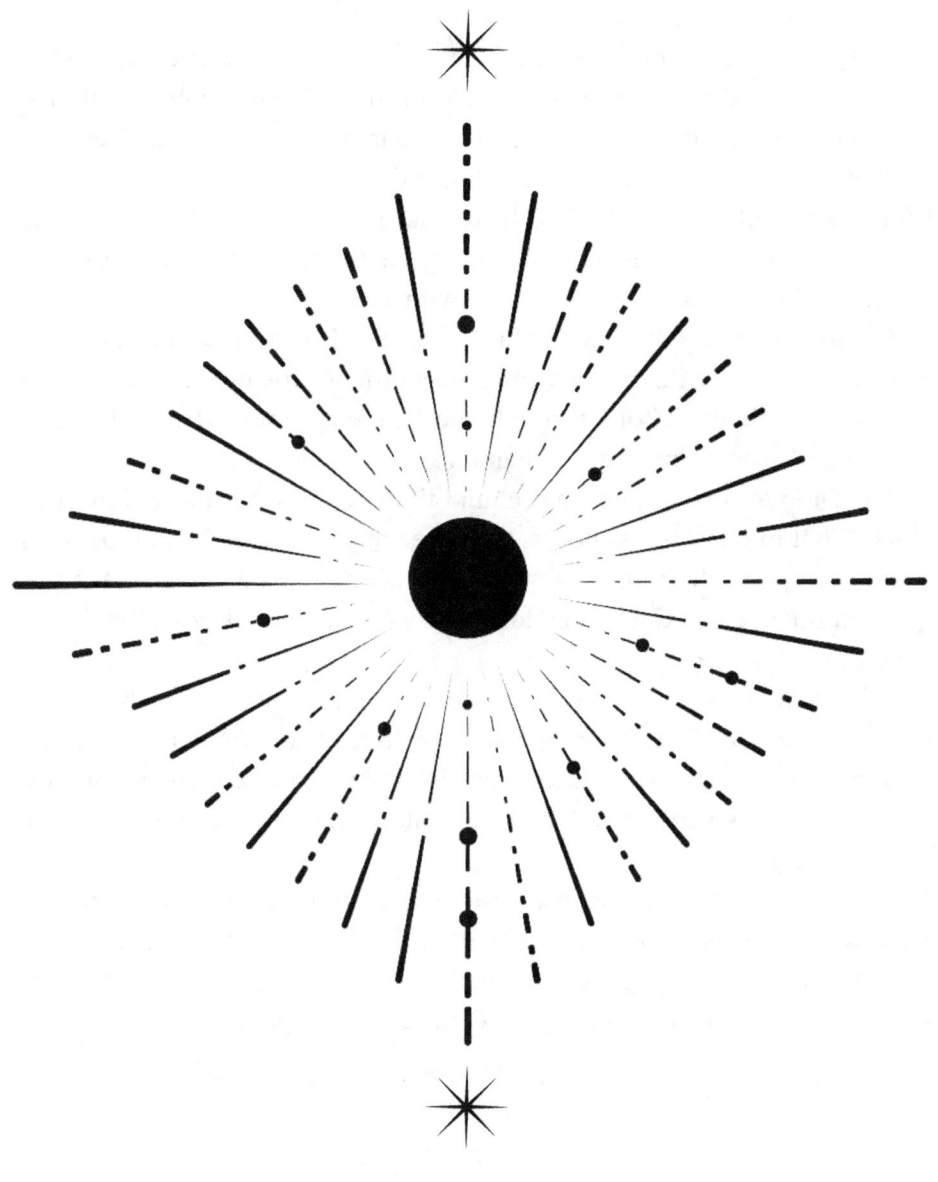

Introduction: While the Embers Are Still Burning

There are moments in life when we are brought to our knees, stripped of every illusion of control, left with nothing but raw, unfiltered love. It is in those moments, when everything is at stake, that we come to understand the true power of love—not as a word, not as a fleeting emotion, but as the most profound force in existence. Love has the power to bridge the seen and the unseen, to defy time, to bend the very fabric of the universe. And sometimes, love is the only thing left standing between life and death.

This story is not fiction. It is not an abstract idea or a poetic expression of hope. It is real. It happened. And for those who have ever questioned whether love has the power to move mountains, to call miracles into existence, let this serve as a testament: it does.

While the Embers Are Still Burning is a story of resilience, of the sacredness of human connection, and of what it means to fight for life—not just with hands and action, but with the heart, with the soul, and with a love so deep it reaches places unseen. It is about a brother who came face to face with the terrifying possibility of losing his sister, about a prayer so fierce it tore through the heavens, about the undeniable presence of something greater than us all.

It is a reminder that life is fragile, and that we do not walk this journey alone. That in our darkest hours, the love we share with those around us is the most powerful thing we will ever possess. And when all else fails—when science and time and odds stand against us—it is love that keeps the embers burning.

This is not just a story; it is a call to remember. To remember that every second is sacred. That every person we love is a gift. That no matter how dark the night, no matter how heavy the burden, love remains. Love fights. Love endures. And love, in its purest form, can pull us back from the edge.

To those who have ever doubted, to those who have ever feared, and to those who have ever stood in the fire of loss—this story is for you.

May it remind you that love never leaves us. As long as the embers are still burning, there is always light waiting to rise again.

While the Embers Are Still Burning

Atticus never believed in miracles. He had grown up in a world where life was carved by effort, where prayer felt like words lost in the wind. But all of that changed the night he nearly lost his sister.

The call came late, piercing the quiet of his house like a siren. His mother's voice, steady but weighted with a fear she was trying to control, carried across the miles. "Lilly is hemorrhaging. The baby is fine, but she's losing too much blood. They've replaced her blood volume seven times already. They ran out, Atticus. They're flying in more, but there's a fifteen-minute window. If it doesn't get here in time... she won't make it."

His world blurred.

Lilly—his best friend, his anchor, the one person who had always been there. The thought of a world without her in it was unbearable. Without hesitation, he booked the first flight out, but the hours between then and now stretched into eternity. He paced, heart pounding, mind racing through every worst-case scenario. The thought that she might not be there when he landed threatened to crush him.

For the first time in his life, he dropped to his knees.

He prayed so close to the bone, so raw it clawed at his soul. It wasn't the kind of prayer he had whispered absentmindedly before. This was desperate, pleading, a prayer that came from the deepest, most primal part of his being. "God, bend the laws of the universe if You have to. Just let her live. Take my strength, take my years, take whatever You must—just don't take her. God, lay in the hands of the surgeon. Let them be steady, let them be guided by something greater than themselves."

He didn't sleep. He whispered her name between prayers, clenching his fists so tightly that his nails cut into his palms. On the plane, he sat motionless, staring at the screen of his phone, dreading the moment he would land and find out if his prayers had been answered or if he had lost the battle before he even arrived.

As the wheels touched the ground, time stood still.

His phone buzzed. His mother's name lit up the screen. His hands shook as he answered. He barely had the strength to say hello.

"She made it. Lilly made it."

His knees gave way.

Right there, in the middle of the crowded terminal, Atticus collapsed, his body surrendering to the weight of relief. Tears streamed down his face. He didn't care who saw. He felt the gravity of the moment press against his chest like ten thousand suns—proof that something greater than him had intervened. For the first time in his life, he knew with absolute clarity—God does exist.

He made it to the hospital as fast as he could. When he finally saw her, she was still unconscious, a ventilator tube down her throat, machines beeping around her fragile frame. He took her hand in his, his thumb running over the softness of her skin, memorizing the warmth, the pulse beneath the surface.

As he sat beside her, the magnitude of what had happened settled in his bones. He had spent so much of his life chasing things—success, money, proving himself. Yet, none of it mattered. Not in that room. Not in the presence of love so deep it defied words.

Then, as the first hints of dawn crept through the window, Lilly stirred. Her eyelids fluttered, her fingers twitched. Then, for the first time since the nightmare began, she opened her eyes.

The doctor came in moments later, assessing her fragile frame, and with a nod, reached for the ventilator tube. "Let's take this out," he said. "She's breathing on her own."

Atticus watched, heart pounding, as the machine was removed, as Lilly took her first breath unassisted. She turned her head slowly, eyes searching, and landed on him. He smiled through the tears that still traced his cheeks.

"You're back," he whispered.

She was weak, her voice barely audible. "The baby?"

"He's perfect. He's waiting for you."

Lilly smiled, and in that moment, Atticus understood something he had never grasped before—love was the most powerful force in existence. It wasn't just a feeling; it was the very essence of life itself. It was what held the world together, what brought light into the darkest places.

Lilly fought her way back to life with a strength that defied logic. Within days, she was sitting up. By the eleventh day, she held her son for the first time, her tears of joy soaking into the tiny blanket that wrapped his perfect little form. Watching her, Atticus felt something inside him shift permanently.

He had witnessed a miracle. He had felt the presence of something greater. He knew, without a doubt, that life—every single breath of it—was worth fighting for.

The sacred power of love revealed itself to him in ways he had never seen before. Love was not just words spoken, not just an idea passed down—it was tangible, unshakable. It was the reason he had prayed until his soul bled. It was the force that had kept Lilly tethered to this world. It was the reason he would never take another moment for granted.

From that moment on, he lived differently. He loved harder, forgave faster, and held his people closer. Because he understood now: life is sacred, love is holy, and the embers of faith will always burn as long as we keep them alive.

Even in the darkest hours, even when the fire seems to dim—there is always light waiting to rise again.

While the embers are still burning, never stop believing in the power of love, of prayer, of life itself.

My life is a testament to the beauty of transformation.

The Weight of Love

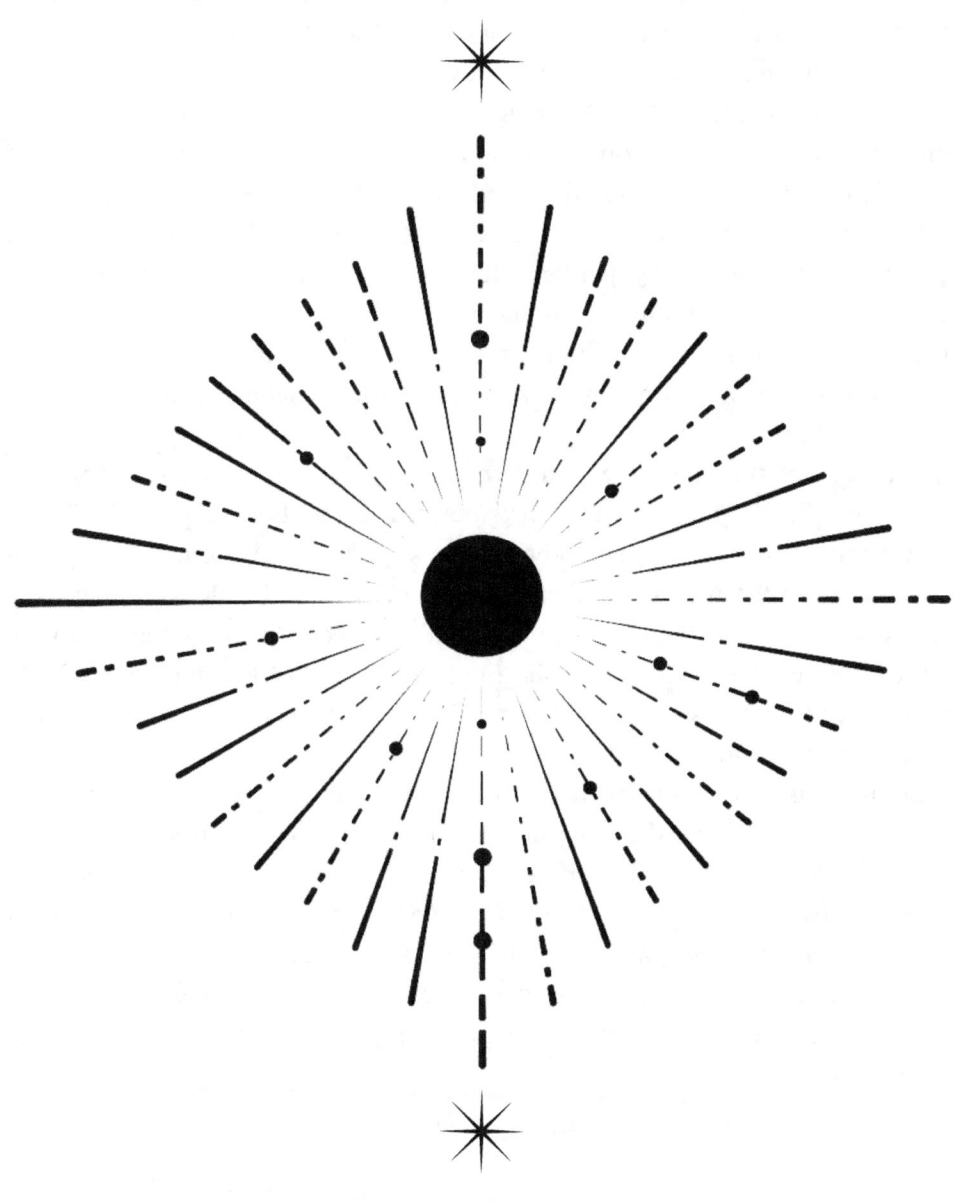

Introduction: The Question That Changes Everything

There comes a moment in every soul's journey when we are faced with a question so profound, so piercing, that it shakes the foundation of everything we believe about love: Am I truly capable of loving unconditionally? It is a question we often avoid, one that lingers quietly beneath the surface of our relationships, waiting for the day we are ready to confront it. Because to love without condition—to truly love—is to stand in the fire of our own expectations and let them burn away, leaving only the raw, unfiltered truth of what love actually is.

I have walked this path. The Weight of Love is not just a story; it is a mirror, a reflection of a journey I have taken myself. It is based on a true experience, one that shattered my illusions about love and, in the same breath, set me free. I once believed I understood love, that I was a compassionate, forgiving person. But when life handed me the ultimate test, I had to face the uncomfortable reality: I had been loving through the lens of conditions, through the filter of expectation. And that is not love—it is attachment, it is longing, it is the need for someone to be different in order for me to feel whole.

So, I ask you now, before you turn the page, to ask yourself the same question: What would it mean for me to love without expectation? Not just when it's easy. Not just when someone loves you back in the way you desire. But in the moments when you feel betrayed, abandoned, or unseen. Could you love then? Could you love without needing an apology, without demanding change, without holding onto the weight of resentment? Could you love for the sake of love itself, even if it asks you to release everything you thought you needed?

This story is not about justification, nor is it about excusing pain. It is about understanding. About seeing another human being in all their flaws and still choosing to love—not because they are deserving in our eyes, but because love, in its purest form, is never about worthiness. It is about being willing to look past the pain, past the unmet expectations, past the disappointment, and into the soul of another, recognizing the divinity in them even when it is buried beneath layers of choices we do not understand.

As you read The Weight of Love, I invite you to open your heart to a new possibility—that love, real love, has nothing to do with control and everything to do with surrender. That maybe, just maybe, the greatest act of love is not in changing another, but in accepting them as they are. And in that acceptance, finding the liberation of your own heart. Because love, when it is truly unconditional, does not bind us—it sets us free.

The Weight of Love

There once was a girl named Rose, who carried within her a love so vast it could have stretched across the sky. Within that same heart, nestled beside the love, was a wound—one carved deep by absence, by longing, by a question that had never been answered. That wound bore the name of her father, Mark.

Mark had been brilliant once. Charismatic, sharp-witted, the kind of man who could command a room with nothing more than a glance and a well-placed word. But none of that had mattered in the end, because his pull to the drink had been greater than the love of his family. It had been greater than his promises, greater than the laughter of his children, greater even than the life he had built. The drink had stolen him away, one sip at a time, until there was nothing left but the shadow of a man who had once been whole.

Rose had been just a child when he left, her mother long gone before him, taking the kids with her, leaving him behind to battle his demons alone. Mark would reappear in fragments—birthday cards that arrived late, Christmas calls that rang hollow. Always, when his money ran dry and the bottle was empty, his voice would slur through the phone, asking for just a little help, a little grace. Yet, no matter how many times he disappeared, Rose carried him with her. She carried him in the half-heart photo she kept in her pocket, a picture of the man he had been before the drink had taken hold.

As Rose grew older, she sought healing. She threw herself into her spiritual journey, peeling back the layers of pain, of abandonment, of resentment that clung to her like vines strangling a tree. She studied, she meditated, she wept. And yet, the wound remained. No matter how much light she poured into herself, there was a part of her still bound in the darkness of his absence.

Then, in her early thirties, she asked herself a question she had spent years avoiding: Am I really practicing unconditional love, or do I only love where it is easy?

The question haunted her. She had spoken of love, of forgiveness, of acceptance, but had she ever truly tested it? Had she ever given love where it was most difficult to give? And so, one day, she picked up the phone. With trembling hands, she dialed the number of the man who had walked away.

When Mark answered, his voice was rough, aged by years of regrets and whiskey. For a moment, neither of them spoke. Then, she asked the question that had lived in her heart since childhood.

"Why did you choose the drink over me? Over your family?"

There was a pause. A long, breathless silence where she felt the weight of decades pressing down on her chest. And then, his voice, quiet but unwavering, came through the line.

"Because I like to drink."

Five words. That was all it took.

Rose had imagined this moment a thousand times. She had imagined rage, excuses, sorrow. She had imagined anything but the simple, brutal truth: Because I like to drink. Not because he was broken, not because he was cursed, not because he was a victim. He had chosen the drink because he liked it. And in that moment, she saw him not as a monster, not as a villain, but as a man—a man with flaws, with desires, with demons he had never learned to slay.

The anger she had held for so long crumbled. The weight of years fell from her shoulders like dust. And in its place, there was only understanding. Not justification, not approval—but understanding. Who was I to claim unconditional love if my love required someone to be who I needed them to be? If love came with terms, was it love at all? Or was it merely another form of control?

She thought about herself, about the things she loved, the things she craved. What if someone told me they would only love me if I abandoned the very thing that made me feel alive? Would that be love? Or would that be a transaction?

Tears welled in her eyes, but for the first time, they were not from pain. They were from release. From the realization that love was never meant to be measured by someone else's ability to meet our expectations. It was meant to be given freely, with no demands, no prerequisites, no strings attached.

Rose inhaled deeply, feeling the rawness of truth settle into her bones. "I forgive you, Dad. Not because you deserve it. Not because you've earned it. But because love isn't something you earn—it's something you give."

Mark didn't respond right away. Maybe he didn't believe her. Maybe he didn't know how to. But it didn't matter. She hadn't said it for him—she had said it for herself.

That night, Rose placed the half-heart photo on her nightstand, no longer a relic of pain, but a symbol of choice. Love was not about changing people. It was not about demanding they be different. It was about seeing them, truly seeing them, and choosing love anyway.

In that choice, she found her own freedom. She understood that true, unconditional love meant releasing the need to control, to fix, to force. It meant meeting people exactly where they were and loving them not despite their shortcomings, but simply because they existed.

She thought back to the years she had spent searching for peace, only to find that it was never in the act of waiting for someone else to change—it was in accepting them as they were. It was in allowing love to be vast enough to hold imperfections, mistakes, and even sorrow. Because real love, the kind that heals, does not demand—it simply is.

For the first time in her life, Rose felt whole. Not because her father had changed, but because she had. Because she had chosen to love, without limits, without conditions, without chains. And in doing so, she had set herself free.

The Dance of Capacity

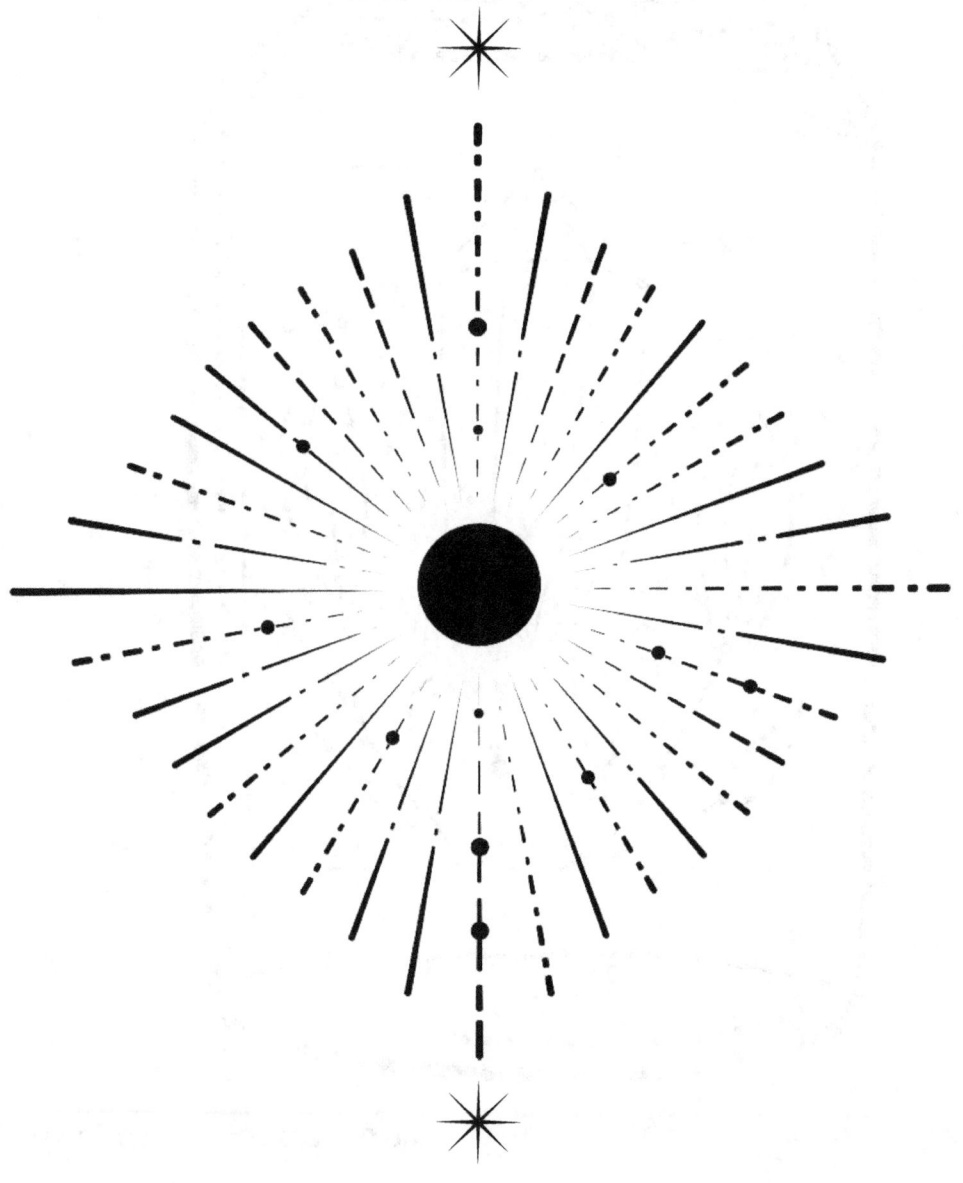

The Dance of Capacity

Introduction: The Dance of Capacity

This story invites you to explore the hidden layers of human connection, revealing profound truths about capacity, consciousness, and grace. It's a tale that gently unfolds the lesson that not everyone in our lives has the ability to meet us where we stand. By observing and understanding the limits of others—without judgment—we discover the power of living in alignment with our own needs and boundaries. This narrative is more than a story; it's a guide to navigating relationships with humility and compassion.

As you journey through these pages, look for the subtle interplay of capacity and consciousness. Notice how the characters reflect the dance we all partake in—the delicate balance of giving and receiving, of meeting others where they are, and of honoring the space we need for ourselves. Let this story be a mirror, reflecting the grace that comes when we let go of expectation and embrace the beauty of human imperfection.

The Dance of Capacity

In the heart of a bustling village nestled within a valley, there lived a woman named Elara. She was known for her boundless compassion and her uncanny ability to see through people—not just their actions, but the layers beneath, where their wounds, joys, and limitations lay hidden. Yet, for all her insight, Elara often found herself frustrated, asking the same silent question: Why can't they see me the way I see them?

One day, after a particularly painful misunderstanding with her closest friend, Elara retreated to the edge of the forest. There, she found solace beneath an ancient oak tree whose roots twisted and coiled like the veins of the earth. As she sat in silence, her tears carving paths down her cheeks, an old man appeared. His presence was as gentle as the breeze yet carried the weight of ageless wisdom.

"You seem burdened," he said, lowering himself onto a root beside her.

Elara hesitated but then poured out her heart. She spoke of her longing for deeper connections, of feeling unseen and unheard, and of the pain that came from expecting others to meet her where she was, only to find them absent.

The man listened patiently, his weathered face unreadable. When she finished, he said, "Come with me."

They walked into the forest, where sunlight filtered through the canopy, casting shifting patterns on the ground. Soon, they came upon a clearing. In the center stood a circle of jars, each filled with water at varying levels. Some were nearly full, while others held only a few drops. The jars were of different shapes and sizes—some cracked, others pristine.

"What do you see?" the man asked.

"Jars," Elara replied, puzzled.

He nodded. "Each of these jars represents a person's capacity. The water inside is what they have to give—their love, empathy, understanding. Notice how some are nearly empty, while others overflow. Yet, even the fullest jar cannot fill another beyond its own size."

Elara knelt beside a jar with a deep crack running down its side. Water seeped out slowly, forming a tiny pool at its base. "And this one?" she asked.

"That jar carries wounds," the man said. "It leaks not out of malice, but because it hasn't been mended. It cannot hold as much as it once could."

Elara's gaze shifted to a small jar with barely a drop of water inside. "And this one?"

"Some jars are simply smaller," he said. "Their capacity was never vast, and that is not their fault."

Elara looked at him, her heart heavy. "But how do I pour from my jar into another when they can't do the same for me?"

The man smiled softly. "That is where grace comes in. To live with grace is to honor each jar for what it is, without demanding it be more. When you expect a small jar to hold what only a larger one can, you set yourself up for disappointment. Observe, Elara. Watch how much each jar can hold, and you will learn how to dance with them. Some will overflow into your life; others will take what they can, and that must be enough."

They stood in silence, the clearing alive with the sound of birds and the rustling of leaves. "But what of my own jar?" Elara asked.

"Your jar must be tended first," he said, his tone firm yet kind. "Fill it with what nourishes you. Protect it from those who take without giving. And when it overflows, let it spill freely, knowing that your abundance is a gift, not a burden. In doing so, you honor both yourself and others."

Elara felt the weight of his words settle into her chest. She thought of her friend who had hurt her, of the times she had given more than she had to give, and of the resentment that had grown from expecting others to meet her where they could not go. In that moment, she understood.

Capacity was not a reflection of worth but of circumstance, history, and being. To meet someone at their capacity was an act of love; to honor her own was an act of self-respect.

The old man began to walk away, but before he disappeared into the trees, he turned back and said, "Remember, Elara, the dance of life is not about filling every jar, but about learning which ones to pour into, and when to step back."

Elara stayed in the clearing a while longer, watching the jars glisten in the sunlight. Each one told a story, not of deficiency, but of individuality. As she made her way back to the village, she carried with her a newfound peace. She no longer needed to demand more from those who couldn't give it, nor did she need to deplete herself trying to bridge the gap.

In the days that followed, Elara became an observer. She saw people as they were, not as she wished them to be. She learned to navigate relationships with humility and grace, meeting others where they stood while honoring her own place in the dance. In doing so, she found that the world, once so heavy, became lighter, filled with the beauty of jars simply being what they were meant to be.

The Prayer That Was Never Lost

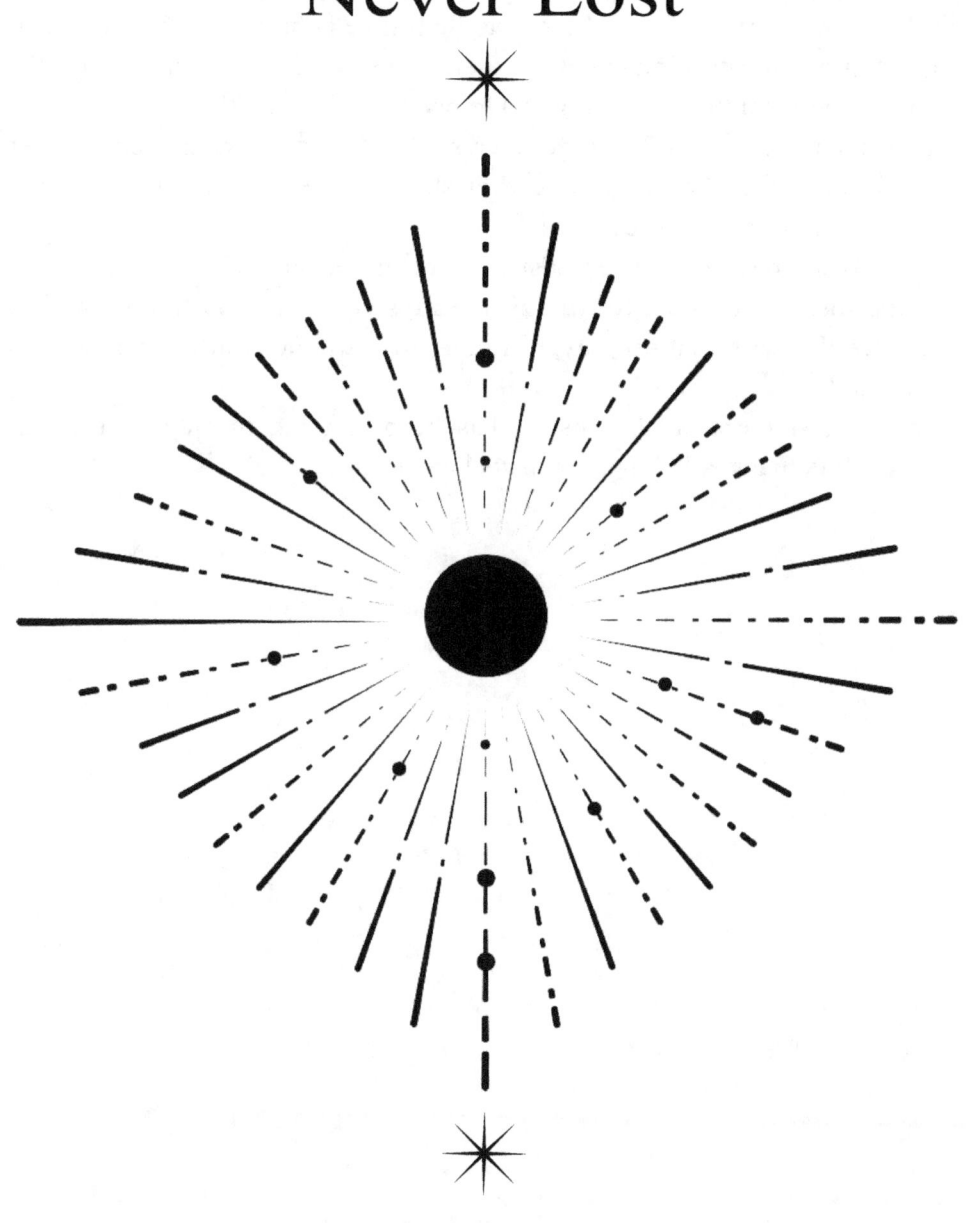

Introduction: The Prayer That Was Never Lost

Have you ever sent out a prayer, a wish, or a plea—only to feel as if it dissolved into silence, unheard and unanswered? Have you ever wondered if your words were swallowed by the vastness of existence, lost in the currents of time?

This story is for those who have ever felt forgotten. It is for the souls who have whispered their hopes into the night and received nothing but stillness in return. It is for the hearts that have ached with the weight of uncertainty, questioning whether their cries for help, their desires for love, or their longing for change have been received at all.

But what if every word you've ever spoken, every thought you've ever sent forth, and every tear you've ever shed was seen? What if nothing—absolutely nothing—was ever lost?

The Prayer That Was Never Lost is more than a story. It is an invitation to step into the unseen, to trust in the mystery of divine timing, and to embrace the truth that no prayer, no longing, and no heartache ever goes unnoticed.

Perhaps, just perhaps, the answer has been arriving in ways you never expected. Perhaps, all along, you have been heard.

The Prayer That Was Never Lost

The boy sat at the edge of the old wooden dock, his bare feet dangling just above the dark water. The sky stretched vast and unbroken above him, a canvas of deep blue velvet speckled with silver light. Orion, his mother had told him once, was the guardian of lost prayers—the ones whispered into the night, unheard by human ears but gathered by the stars.

Caleb had always believed in prayers, though lately, they felt like whispers in an empty room. He had prayed for his father to come home, prayed for his mother to stop crying at night, prayed for the weight in his chest to lift, even just for a moment. Yet the world remained unchanged, as if his words dissolved before reaching anything that could catch them.

He closed his eyes and whispered again, "Are you even listening?" The night only answered with the gentle lapping of water against the dock. He sighed and pulled his knees to his chest, feeling the sting of loneliness press against his ribs.

"Prayers are not always answered the way we expect."

The voice startled him. Caleb turned to see an old man standing at the end of the dock, hands tucked into the folds of his long coat. His face was lined with years, but his eyes held something ageless, like the hush before dawn.

"Who are you?" Caleb asked, his voice small against the vastness of the night.

The man smiled, stepping closer. "A watcher, a listener—someone who has been where you are now."

Caleb hesitated. "And where is that?"

"Lost in the idea that silence means no one is listening."

Caleb looked away. "I don't think my prayers matter. They just disappear."

The man knelt beside him and dipped a hand into the water. "Tell me, what happens when you throw a stone into a lake?"

Caleb glanced at the water. "It makes ripples."

"And do you see every ripple it makes? Do you know how far they travel?"

Caleb shook his head. "No."

The man nodded. "Yet they keep moving, far beyond what your eyes can follow. Your prayers are the same.

Just because you cannot see where they go does not mean they have vanished." Caleb sat with this for a moment. "But if they reach something, why does nothing change?"

The man's expression softened, as if he had heard this question a thousand times before. "Ah, but how do you know nothing is changing?"

Caleb bit his lip. He had no answer for that. The man continued, "Every thought you send out, every word you whisper, every hope you carry in your heart—it is seen. It is heard. No moment of your existence is overlooked. Sometimes what we ask for comes in ways we do not expect. Sometimes it arrives long after we have given up looking for it. And sometimes, the prayer is not about changing the world, but about changing you."

A lump formed in Caleb's throat. "So you're saying... my prayers do matter?"

"Every single one." The man rose to his feet, brushing off his coat. "The Universe is always listening, even when you feel forgotten. You were never alone, and you never will be."

A gust of wind moved over the water, cool against Caleb's skin. He wanted to ask the man more, but when he looked up, he was gone; as if he had never been there at all.

Caleb sat in the stillness, his heart beating slow and steady. He tilted his head toward the stars and whispered once more—not in doubt this time, but in trust.

The night stretched quiet and vast, but something felt different. The weight he had carried for so long was no longer his to bear alone. A warmth settled in his chest, spreading like the first light of dawn breaking over the horizon.

In that moment, Caleb understood—prayers were never wasted. Some were answered in the form of quiet strength, some in the unfolding of time, and some in ways beyond human understanding.

He no longer needed to see to believe. He no longer needed proof. He simply knew.

Somewhere beyond sight, beyond sound, beyond all that the world could measure, something heard him.

It always had.

It always would.

101
Affirmations for Forgotten Magnificence

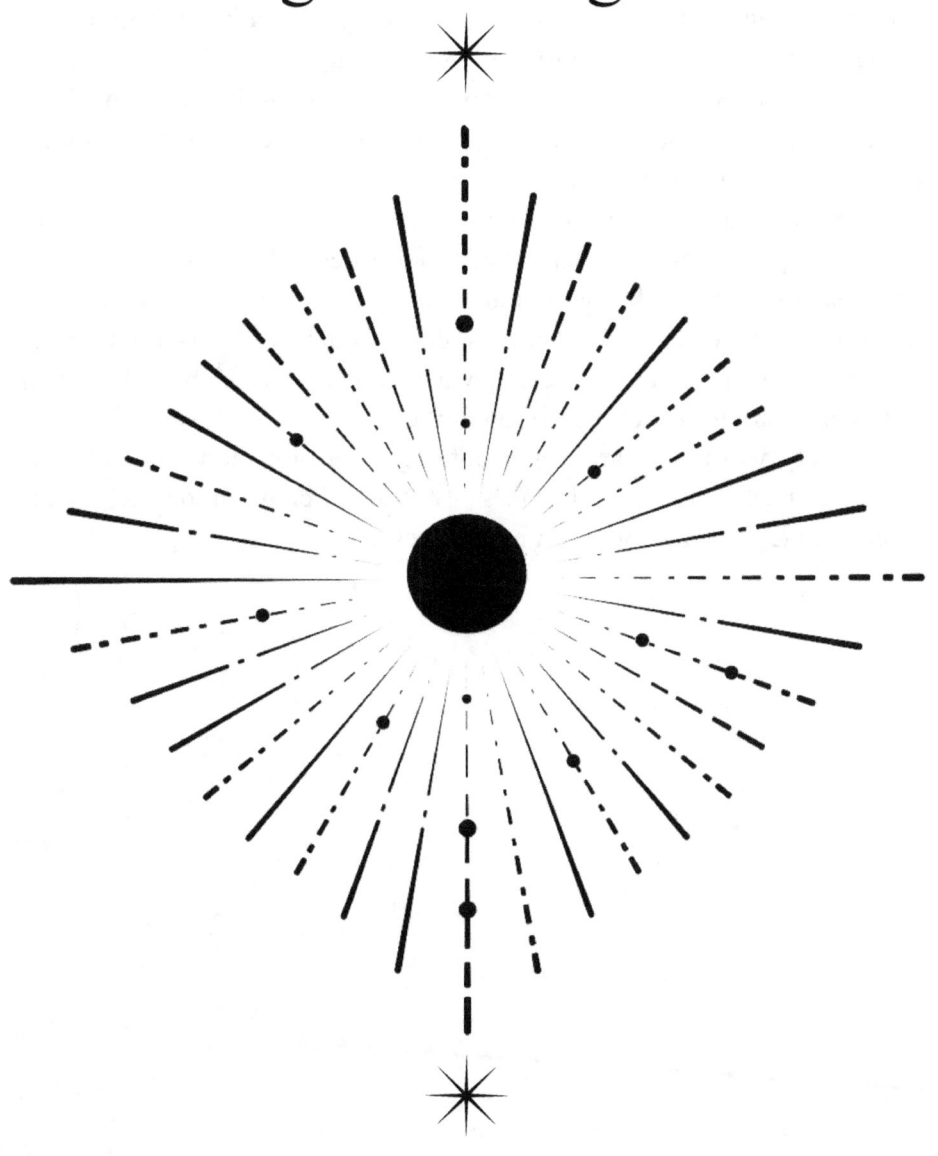

The Power of Sacred Words

Within you lies a brilliance untouched by time, a magnificence that has never been blemished—only buried beneath the weight of the world. These affirmations are more than words; they are sacred invocations, a remembering of the vastness, power, and divinity that resides within you. They are the language of your soul speaking itself back into wholeness.

When spoken with intention, these words become more than mere sentences; they transform into living energy, vibrating through your being, shifting the very fabric of your reality. They are mantras of awakening, prayers of reclamation, and declarations of truth. With each affirmation, you are realigning with the essence of who you have always been—boundless, luminous, sovereign.

Let these affirmations be your anchor in moments of doubt, your guide when the path seems unclear, and your torch when the world feels dark. Speak them with conviction, whisper them in stillness, or write them into existence. Use them as daily rituals of self-honoring, as sacred reminders that you were never meant to shrink, but to expand—never meant to forget, but to remember.

With every word, you are not becoming—you are returning. You are stepping back into the fullness of your being, into the sacred remembrance of your forgotten magnificence.

Affirmations for Forgotten Magnificence

I honor the magnificence that resides within me.

My soul is radiant with divine light.

I embrace the beauty of my unique journey.

I release the need for external validation and trust my inner worth.

I am aligned with the highest version of myself.

I step into my power with grace and humility.

The truth of my being is infinite love.

I am deeply connected to the divine wisdom within me.

My capacity for growth is boundless.

I choose to see myself through the eyes of love.

I honor the lessons hidden within life's challenges.

I am a living legacy of grace, grit, and glory.

The light within me cannot be dimmed.

I embrace my shadow as a sacred part of my wholeness.

I have the courage to release what no longer serves me.

My vulnerability is a strength, not a weakness.

I am deserving of peace and fulfillment.

I allow myself to rest in the stillness of my soul.

I am a vessel of healing for myself and others.

Every experience shapes me into a more aligned version of myself.

My worth is innate and unshakable.

I honor my emotions as sacred messengers.

I forgive myself for past mistakes and welcome new beginnings.

The divine flows through every part of my being.

I trust the timing of my unfolding.

I choose love over fear in every decision I make.

My heart is open to giving and receiving love.

I release expectations and accept others for who they are.

I am safe to be my authentic self.

I embrace the sacred dance of capacity and grace.

I hold space for others while honoring my own boundaries.

My presence is enough; I am enough.

I am anchored in the infinite, unshakable peace within me.

My soul is a reflection of divine magnificence.

I am resilient and capable of rising above life's storms.

I trust in the divine wisdom that guides my path.

I am free to create a life aligned with my deepest truth.

I see challenges as opportunities for transformation.

I radiate love, light, and compassion in all that I do.

My scars tell the story of my strength and courage.

I am the author of my life's sacred narrative.

I surrender my fears and trust in divine protection.

My joy is a holy act of rebellion against despair.

I honor the sacred duality of my light and shadow.

The capacity of my soul is limitless and expanding.

I walk with grace, grounded in my divine identity.

I release judgment of myself and others and choose understanding.

I am in harmony with the flow of the universe.

My life is a testament to the beauty of transformation.

I carry the forgotten magnificence of humanity within me.

I am the keeper of a sacred legacy, born from love and divinity.

My soul speaks truths that the world has yet to hear.

I rise above the dictates of society and reclaim my forgotten power.

Every breath I take is a testament to my resilience.

I am whole, even in my brokenness.

The universe moves through me, creating beauty in my existence.

I hold the key to unlocking the divine wisdom within me.

My shadow is not my enemy but a guide to deeper understanding.

My capacity to love grows as I learn to love myself.

I am a vessel of infinite possibilities and divine creation.

The magnificence I seek has always been within me.

I trust the process of shedding old identities to reveal my true self.

I am a living reminder that light and shadow coexist in harmony.

I choose to stand in my truth, even when the world does not understand.

My worth is not defined by what I do, but by who I am.

I am rooted in grace and rise in glory.

My wounds are portals to the deepest healing and transformation.

I walk in alignment with my highest calling.

The divine blueprint of my soul is unfolding perfectly.

I honor the lessons that pain and joy bring into my life.

I am both student and teacher in the sacred journey of life.

The magnificence of creation is reflected in my being.

I am a masterpiece, constantly evolving in beauty and depth.

I surrender my fears and embrace the freedom of divine trust.

My authenticity is my most sacred offering to the world.

I hold space for my growth with patience and compassion.

I see beyond the illusions of separation and embrace unity.

My life is a reflection of divine purpose and grace.

I am a mirror of the divine, reflecting love and truth.

The depth of my soul cannot be measured by the superficial.

I am free to rewrite the story of my life with courage and love.

My spirit is unbreakable, even in the face of trials.

I release the need to be understood and rest in self-awareness.

I am a guardian of my energy, giving only from my overflow.

I honor the capacity of others without diminishing my own.

I am the architect of my destiny, guided by divine wisdom.

The sacred within me calls forth the sacred in others.

I am at peace with the unknown, for it is where magic resides.

I embrace the fullness of my humanity and divinity.

My voice carries the power of truth and transformation.

I honor the divine cycles of creation, destruction, and rebirth within me.

My magnificence is not diminished by others' inability to see it.

I am not bound by the limitations of others' perceptions.

My soul's journey is sacred, and I walk it with reverence.

I release comparison and celebrate the uniqueness of my path.

I am a reflection of divine light, infinite and eternal.

I am deeply connected to the wisdom of the universe.

I honor the divine timing of my transformation.

I am both the question and the answer, the seeker and the found.

I release the weight of others' expectations and embrace my authentic self.

The forgotten magnificence within me rises with every act of self-love.

Forgotten Magnificence
Conclusion

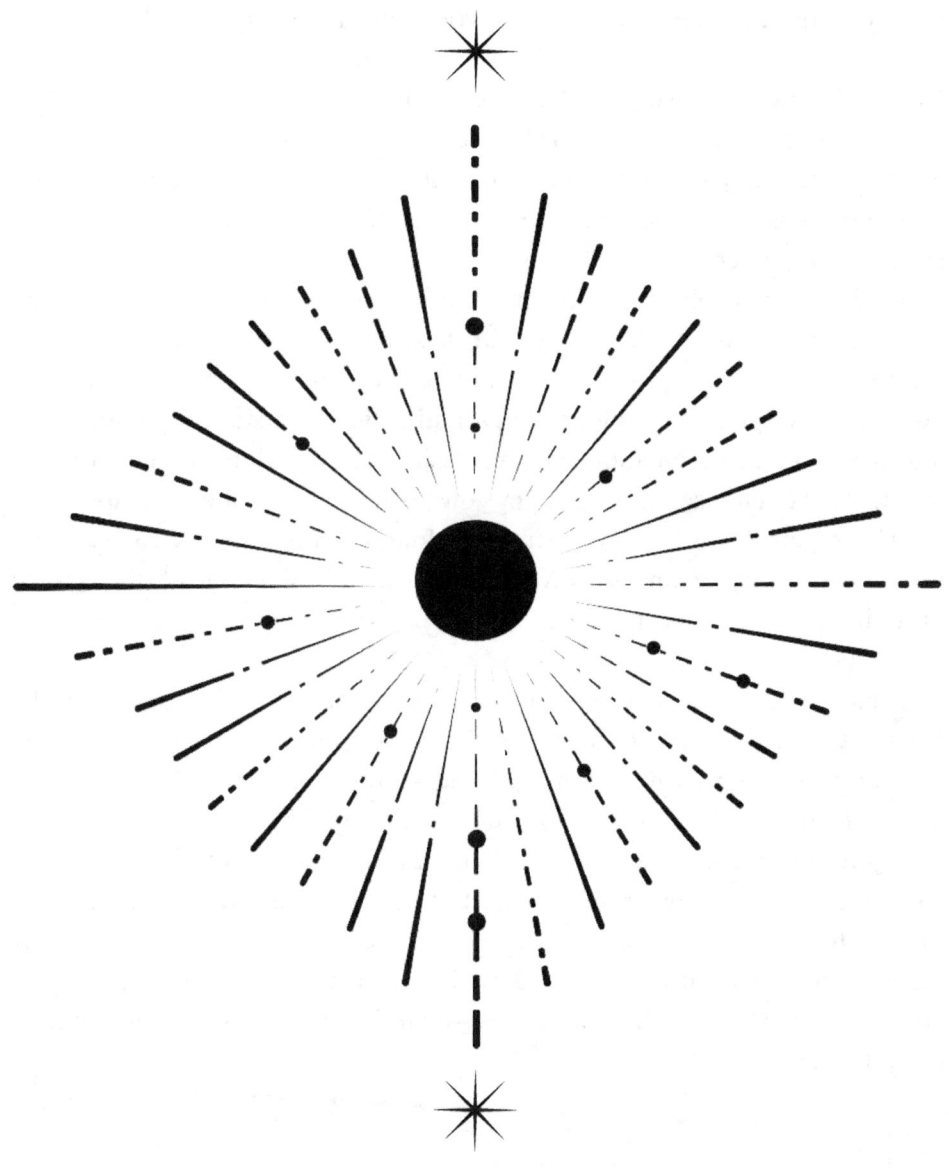

The Magnificence That Was Always Within

To you, the reader, who has journeyed through these pages—thank you. Thank you for your willingness to sit with these words, to reflect on your own sacred truth, and to allow the possibility that you were never broken to begin with.

This book was never about giving you something outside of yourself. It was always about pointing you back to what was already within—the vast, untouched magnificence that you may have forgotten but never lost.

You were never meant to live as a fractured version of yourself, doubting your place in this world. Life itself is waiting to inspire you, to breathe through you, to remind you that you are not here by accident. The entire cosmos conspired for you to be exactly who you are—whole, radiant, and powerful beyond measure.

Stand in your wholeness. Do not wait for permission to be who you were always meant to be. The world does not need more people hiding their light, hesitating in fear, or believing they are unworthy. The world needs more of you—unapologetically, authentically, beautifully you.

You are a force of creation, an expression of something divine. Every moment you choose to step into your truth, you ignite a spark that lights the path for others. You are not alone on this journey. Every soul you meet, every connection you make, is a reflection of the great unfolding, a reminder that we are all part of something greater than ourselves.

You have walked through darkness and still found the courage to seek the light. You have faced doubt, yet here you stand, open to the infinite possibility of your own becoming. That is no small thing. That is grace. That is resilience. That is magnificence in its purest form.

The journey ahead is yours to shape. Let yourself live fully, not as someone waiting to be made whole, but as one who already is. Let life move through you, inspire you, and reveal to you the boundless potential that has always existed within. You are the beating heart of creation, a masterpiece in motion, ever-evolving and expanding into more of yourself.

So go forward, not seeking to be fixed, but embracing the magnificence that is already inside you. Let your life be your offering, your presence be your gift, and your truth be your guide. Let yourself be seen, be heard, be felt—not as something incomplete, but as the whole and sacred being that you are.

And when you are done with this book, pass it on. Let someone else hold these words when they need them most. Let this be a ripple, a reminder, a beacon of the light that cannot be extinguished. Let this book live on as a testament to the truth—that you were never broken. You were always whole.

May you walk forward with courage, with love, and with the unshakable knowing that your existence is a gift to this world. May you live boldly, love deeply, and remember always—the magnificence that was never lost.

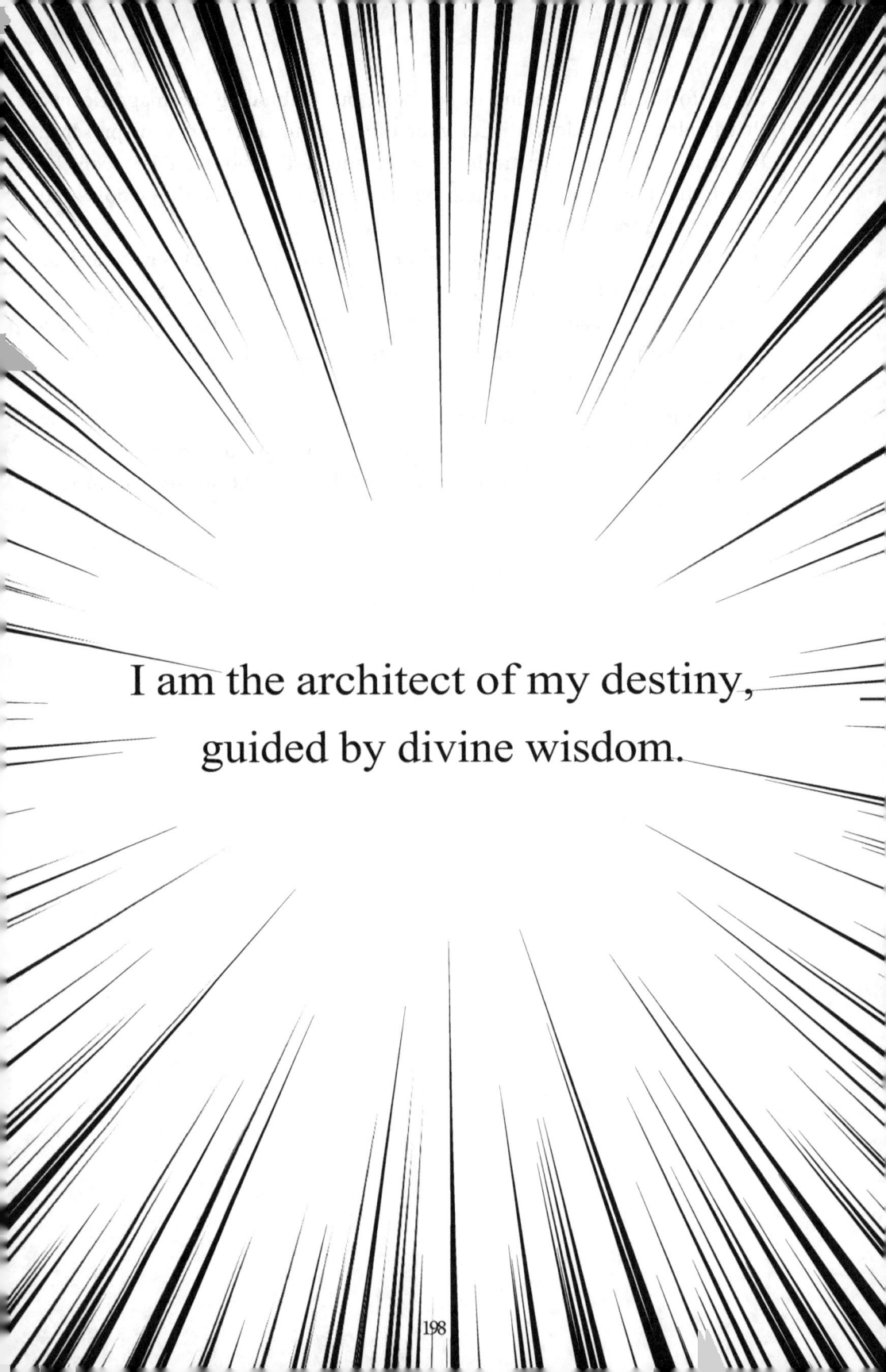

I am the architect of my destiny, guided by divine wisdom.

www.ingramcontent.com/pod-product-compliance
Lightning Source LLC
Chambersburg PA
CBHW070425010526
44118CB00014B/1903